Politics in Britain
Democracy in Action?

compiled and edited
by
David Beal

Berlin · München · Wien · Zürich · New York

Viewfinder

Topics

Politics in Britain

Democracy in Action?

Herausgeber:
Prof. Dr. Peter Freese

Autor:
David Beal, M. A.

Projekt-Team:
David Beal, M. A.
Dr. Peter Dines, Cert. Ed.
Prof. Dr. Hanspeter Dörfel
Prof. Dr. Peter Freese
Dr. Carin Freywald
Prof. Dr. Harald Husemann
Michael Mitchell, M. A.
Dr. Michael Porsche
StR Detlef Rediker
StD Dr. Peter-J. Rekowski
OStR Dr. Annegret Schrick
OStR Ekkehard Sprenger
OStD Dr. Horst Steur
Donald Turner, M. A.

Redaktion:
Dr. Annegret Pago, in Zusammenarbeit mit der Verlagsredaktion
Christina Maria Hackenberg, M. A.

Projektleitung Grafik:
Beate Andler

Gestaltung und Desktop-Publishing:
Barbara Slowik, Atelier S., München

Titelfoto:
Gareth Boden, Herford

Umwelthinweis: Gedruckt auf chlorfrei gebleichtem Papier.

1. Auflage 1996

© 1996 Langenscheidt ELT GmbH, München

Das Werk und seine Teile sind urheberrechtlich geschützt. Jede Verwertung in anderen als den gesetzlich zugelassenen Fällen bedarf deshalb der vorherigen schriftlichen Einwilligung des Verlages.

Druck: Mediengruppe Universal, München
Printed in Germany

ISBN 13: 978-3-526-50756-7

ISBN 10: 3-526-50756-2

Introduction

Politics can be an exciting subject. Serious, complex, often amusing, unpredictable, and dynamic, it affects the daily lives of every one of us even if we choose to ignore it. In a sense, though, it is impossible to ignore politics completely since we are all the objects of political activity. Schools and universities, health services, housing, employment, transport, the environment, and old age are all influenced by political ideology, the political system, and the actions of politicians. In this, human beings have much in common. We all have to reconcile different interests and viewpoints. We contribute our views in the process of policy and decision-making which sets priorities in the distribution of wealth, income and national resources. And we have to organise the institutions which carry out these aims.

What we today have come to recognize as the democratic tradition is the result of historical events and changes in social structures over a long period of time. Of all the various political systems that have emerged in the twentieth century, the British has been one of the most influential. It has in the past been seen in an overwhelmingly positive light and has been taken by many as exemplary. Its political institutions have a long and unbroken history (the mother of parliaments; a monarchy going back to A.D. 802), its political culture is characterised by fair play and compromise, tradition is balanced by an ability to change, the rule of law and democratic traditions (*Magna Carta, Habeas Corpus*) have put down roots which make authoritarian or even dictatorial regimes appear unthinkable, and it seems based not on abstract political philosophies but on pragmatic and realistic attitudes.

This collection of fourteen texts, dating from 1215 to 1994, will enable you to judge how far these views are valid. It covers the historical dimension, not only through important documents such as *Magna Carta*, but also by showing the efforts over 600 years of ordinary people to influence public affairs through peaceful and less peaceful means. It deals with the structure of the contemporary British political system, the political parties, their history and their ideologies, and the electoral system. Finally, it focuses on political persuasion and manipulation through advertising, a political speech and an interview. The wide variety of texts represented here, both verbal – newspaper articles, fictional diary, poem, exposition, speech, interview – and non-verbal – charts, cartoons, photographs, advertisements – will help you acquire skills in their analysis and gain an insight into British attitudes towards politics.

All texts and study aids in this book have been scrutinised by the project team and numerous practising teachers. In this context we should also like to thank Dr. Ingrid Benecke, Stuttgart; Stefanie Marx, Potsdam; Thomas Meyer, Duisburg; Dr. Astrid Scheuerer-Willmar, Chieming, and Rolf Wüst, Neuwied, for their valuable help in ascertaining the effectiveness of the materials.

David Beal

Contents

		Study Texts	Study Aids
	Politics in Britain: *Democracy in Action?*	p. 1	p. 26
1	Excerpts from *Magna Carta**	p. 2	p. 26
2	Antony Jay: "A 'United' Kingdom: The Role of the Monarchy"*	p. 3	p. 28
	Satire		p. 28
3	The Myth of the 'Unwritten' British Constitution*	p. 5	p. 29
4	Roger Woddis: "Helping with Enquiries"	p. 6	p. 31
5	"How Representative Is Parliament?"*	p. 7	p. 33
6	Jonathan Lynn and Antony Jay: "The Smokescreen"	p. 9	p. 34
7	*The Story of the Tolpuddle Martyrs*	p. 11	p. 36
8	"Should We Ban Strikes in Key Public Services?" *The Observer*, 28 August 1994	p. 14	p. 38
9	Political Advertising*:	p. 16	p. 41
	An Advertisement for the Conservative Party	p. 16	
	An Advertisement for the Labour Party	p. 17	
10	"Portrait of the Electorate", *The Sunday Times*, 12 April 1992	p. 18	p. 43
11	"Electoral Reform: Which System Is Best?"* *The Guardian*, 8 April 1992	p. 19	p. 44
	"Election Results"*, taken from *The Independent on Sunday*, 12 April 1992	p. 20	
12	An Interview with John Major: What do the Conservatives Stand for?*	p. 21	p. 45
13	A Political Speech: Tony Benn on Britain and Europe*	p. 22	p. 46
14	"A Democratic Checklist"*, *Bite the Ballot*, Supplement to the *New Statesman & Society*, 29 April 1994	p. 23	p. 48
	Glossary		p. 49

Politics in Britain
Democracy in Action?

Politics is "a strife of interests masquerading as principles".
Ambrose Bierce, *The Devil's Dictionary* (1911)

Politics is "essential to human freedom ... something to be valued as a pearl beyond price in the history of the human condition".
Bernard Crick, *In Defence of Politics* (1992)

"I think it is very dangerous for people to believe politics is irrelevant because the people who hold the power do not believe that."
Wal Hobson, political activist, quoted from *Is Democracy Working*, ed. Sheila Browne (1986)

Politics is the process by which it is decided "who gets what, when and how".
Bill Coxall, *Contemporary British Politics* (1991)

"Politics is not the art of the possible. It consists in choosing between the disastrous and the unpalatable."
J. K. Galbraith (1969)

David 'Screaming Lord' Sutch presents an election poster for the Official Monster Raving Loony Party during the April 1992 election campaign. It shows the leaders of the three main parties wearing fools' caps. In that election the Official Monster Raving Loony Party fielded 30 candidates who obtained a total of 10,437 votes out of about 32 million votes cast. – The Independent.

1 Excerpts from *Magna Carta**

Magna Carta, signed by King John at Runnymede near Windsor in June 1215, forms together with the Petition of Right (1629) and the Bill of Rights (1689) what has been called the 'Bible of the British Constitution'. King John was forced to sign the Charter by barons who had rebelled against him. The causes of their rebellion were John's demands for money to finance foreign wars, his arbitrary methods of collecting taxation, and the brutal treatment of those who refused payment. *Magna Carta* – parts of it are still the law of the land – was the first step in establishing the rule of law in Britain. 14 of its 63 articles are printed here.
G.R.C. Davies, *Magna Carta* (London: The British Library, 1985), pp. 23-28.

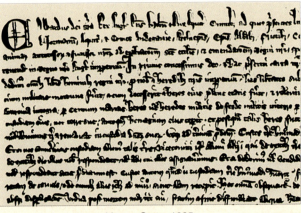

Magna Carta, 1225

John, by the grace of God King of England, Lord of Ireland, Duke of Normandy and Aquitaine, and Count of Anjou, to his archbishops, bishops, abbots, earls, barons, justices, foresters, sheriffs, stewards, servants, and to all his officials and loyal subjects, Greetings. To all free men of our kingdom we have also granted, for us and our heirs, all the liberties written out below, to have and to keep for them and their heirs, of us and our heirs: [...]

(8) No woman shall be compelled to marry, so long as she wishes to remain without a husband. But she must give security that she will not marry without royal consent, if she holds her lands of the Crown, or without the consent of whatever other lord she may hold them of.

(12) No 'scutage' or 'aid' may be levied in our kingdom without its general consent, unless it be for the ransom of our person, to make our eldest son a knight, and (once) to marry our eldest daughter. For these purposes only a reasonable 'aid' may be levied. [...]

(13) The city of London shall enjoy all its ancient liberties and free customs, both by land and by water. We also will grant that all other cities, boroughs, towns, and ports shall enjoy all their liberties and free customs.

(14) To obtain the general consent of the realm for the assessment of an 'aid' – except in the three cases specified above – or a 'scutage', we will cause the archbishops, bishops, abbots, earls, and greater barons to be summoned individually by letter. [...]

(15) In future we will allow no one to levy an 'aid' from his free men, except to ransom his person, to make his eldest son a knight, and (once) to marry his eldest daughter. For these purposes only a reasonable 'aid' may be levied.

(16) No man shall be forced to perform more service for a knight's fee, or other free holding of land, than is due from it.

(20) For a trivial offence, a free man shall be fined only in proportion to the degree of his offence, and for a serious offence correspondingly, but not so heavily as to deprive him of his livelihood.
In the same way, a merchant shall be spared his merchandise, and a husbandman the implements of his husbandry, if they fall upon the mercy of a royal court. None of these fines shall be imposed except by the assessment on oath of reputable men of the neighbourhood.

(23) No town or person shall be forced to build bridges over rivers except those with an ancient obligation to do so.

(30) No sheriff, royal official, or other person shall take horses or carts for transport from any free man, without his consent.

(31) Neither we nor any royal official will take wood for our castle, or for any other purpose, without the consent of the owner.

(35) There shall be standard measures of wine, ale, and corn [...] throughout the kingdom. There shall also be a standard width of dyed cloth [...] Weights are to be standardised similarly.

(38) In future no official shall place a man on trial upon his own unsupported statement, without producing credible witnesses to the truth of it.

(39) No free man shall be seized or imprisoned, or stripped of his rights or possessions, or outlawed or exiled, or deprived of his standing in any other way, nor will we proceed with force against him, or send others to do so, except by the lawful judgement of his equals or by the law of the land.

(40) To no one will we sell, to no one deny or delay right or justice.

Given by our hand in the meadow that is called Runnymede, between Windsor and Staines, on the fifteenth day of June in the seventeenth year of our reign.

2 Antony Jay
"A 'United' Kingdom: The Role of the Monarchy"*

The monarchy as an institution and the members of the royal family themselves have come under increasing criticism since the end of the 1980s. Doubts have been expressed about the relevance of the monarchy in modern Britain; members of the royal family have been criticised for their extravagant lifestyles; the marital problems of Charles and Andrew have made people doubt whether the royal family are moral examples to the nation, and many people think the royal family get too much money from the state. In a booklet entitled *The Monarchy*, published to accompany a television series of the same name, Antony Jay makes this defence of the monarchy. – Antony Jay, "A 'United' Kingdom", *The Monarchy*, ed. Laura Murrell (London: London Weekend Television, 1992), pp. 18f.

The state opening of parliament:
The Queen reads a speech written by ministers.

> **O**ur far-flung empire imposed new rules
> And lasted a century or so
> Until engrossed in football pools
> We shrugged our shoulders and let it go.
>
> **B**ut old traditions are hard to kill
> However knocked about they've been.
> And it's still, for some, an authentic thrill
> To go to London to see the Queen ...
>
> Noel Coward

Why do we need a hereditary monarch? Most states manage with an appointed or elected President, and a President could open and dissolve parliament, sign its acts, welcome visiting Heads of State and perform all the other legal and ceremonial functions at present discharged by the Queen.

The truth is that if that was all the monarchy was for, we would not need a Royal Family. But the British system of government is built on the recognition that a state is more than a collection of individuals, a system of laws and an area of land. It is also a focus of the emotions of a people; it expresses our sense of nationhood, and it engages our pride, our patriotism and our loyalty. When British teams do well in international championships and when British athletes win Gold Medals at the Olympics, we all walk a bit taller. And that emotional involvement in our country, that national pride, is as much a part of the totality of Britain as our legal and political system. That pride and patriotism find their expression, their focus and their symbol in the person of the Sovereign, just as our disagreements about how to run schools and hospitals, how much to raise in taxes and how to spend it, find their focus and expression in the conflict between the political parties in Parliament. The two together balance each other neatly: Parliament portrays public life as a battlefield, the monarchy portrays it as a family circle.

It is difficult for an elected President to represent all the nation. At times, he will be almost unknown to most of the people. At others, he will be a party politician identified with one faction, and will have been regularly voted against by getting on for half the electorate. By contrast, a hereditary monarch will have been known to all the nation from birth, will be politically impartial, and will have spent all his or her life before Coronation apprenticed to the job. Certainly it is hard to think of a less democratic system than hereditary monarchy; on the other hand, the office confers very little power, though much influence and status. Democracy has to be balanced against continuity.

The British system of government recognises that there are not one but two roles to be performed by the Head of State: one is the formal, constitutional, ceremonial role of presiding over and authorising the activities of the government; the other is the personal, emotional role of being Head of the Nation, the focus of the people's pride and loyalty and affection, the embodiment of their sense of nationhood. When these two roles are combined in a single institution, a single family and a single office, then people are simultaneously focusing these emotions on the constitutional state; they are confirming and supporting the legitimacy of the legal, political and economic system which regulates their daily lives.

Because of this, the monarchy is an important force for unity in Britain – perhaps the single most important force. We have been lucky enough to maintain that national unity for centuries, which makes it easy to take it for granted. But we only have to look at Yugoslavia [...] to see what can happen when national unity is broken, when significant groups of people no longer feel any sense of belonging to the state under whose laws they live.

How long will the British monarchy last? It has been with us a thousand years, but it could be abolished tomorrow: it is Parliament, not the Queen, which is sovereign. The monarchy's roots are not in bygone centuries but in the hearts of the people, and in the end it is the will of the British people that will determine its fate. Perhaps it is not that undemocratic after all.

The royal family on the balcony of Buckingham Palace in happier times?

A satirical view of the royal family

3 The Myth of the 'Unwritten' British Constitution*

Constitutions are rules governing the structure, organisation and procedure of a state or any other body such as a university, football club or a scientific society. It used to be said that Britain did not have a constitution. Later when this view was seen to be wrong it was common to describe the British constitution as unwritten. Now it is clear that this interpretation is also in error.

> Can, then, Mr Burke produce the English Constitution? If he cannot, we may fairly conclude that, though it has been much talked about, no such thing as a Constitution exists ... — *Thomas Paine*

The British Constitution

Statute law and EU law

1 Statute law is by far the most important part of the constitution. It consists of Acts of Parliament which 5 regulate the following matters: the composition of the electorate (Representation of the People Acts, 1832-1928), the relationship 10 between the House of Commons and the House of Lords (Parliament Act, 1911), between the component parts of the United 15 Kingdom (Act of Union with Scotland, 1707), between the Crown and parliament (Bill of Rights, 1689), between the U.K. 20 and the EU (European Community Act, 1972), and between the state and the individual citizen (*Habeas Corpus* Act, 25 1679).

Common law

This means case law and custom, laws which have been made by the courts or which have grown up 30 as accepted practice over the years. The sovereignty of parliament is based on common law, as is the royal prerogative in the 35 appointment of ministers, the dissolution of parliament, the power of pardon, and the award of honours.

Works of Authority

40 Works written by constitutional experts are often consulted in cases of doubt as there is no British Supreme Court such as exists 45 in the United States or Germany.

Conventions

Conventions are informal rules which are considered binding by those who 50 operate the constitution, but which are not enforced by the law courts. It is a convention of the British constitution that the mon-55 arch must appoint as prime minister a person who has the confidence of the House of Commons. In normal circumstances 60 this is the leader of the majority party. It is also a convention that the monarch must assent to laws passed by the House of 65 Commons.

As can be seen from this chart the British constitution is partly written. It would therefore be more accurate to describe it as uncodified, i.e. not set out in a single document like those of Germany or the United States.

Politics in Britain

4 Roger Woddis
"Helping with Enquiries"

After writing a letter to his local paper about the poll tax and the Peasants' Revolt of 1381, Dave Roddy of Royston, near Oldham, Lancashire, was visited by two plainclothes policemen who warned him, over a cup of tea, that he might be inciting trouble. Roger Woddis wrote a satirical poem about this incident.
New Statesman & Society, 23 March 1990, p. 8.

Wat Tyler (left foreground) killed at Smithfields by the Mayor of London in the presence of the rebellious peasants he led

The mob – most of them poor and unemployed from the East End of London – take their revenge on the wealthy in the West End as they smash club windows in St. James's Street (1886).

Wat Tyler, he came up from Kent 1
   To talk about a tax
And ask the king, the peasants' friend
   To lift it from their backs.
The Mayor of London drew his sword 5
   And stopped him in his tracks.

A serf in 1381,
   Who dared to stand his ground
Could not expect to die in bed,
   As Wat at Smithfields found. 10
Today they simply note complaints
   And send the coppers round.

"Good morning, sir," they said to Dave,
   As nice as nice can be.
"We've called to have a little chat – 15
   Assuming that you're free."
They were so sweet, they had no need
   Of sugar in their tea.

They cautioned him, but being kind
   Did not detain him long. 20
Dave Roddy led no peasant band
   A hundred thousand strong;
But twenty million on the march
   Can't all of them be wrong.

Poll tax rioters in London 1990

Politics in Britain

5 "How Representative Is Parliament?"

> Jim Hacker, the prime minister in the satirical BBC television series *Yes Prime Minister*, says: "Being an MP is a vast subsidised ego trip. It is a job which needs no qualifications, it has no compulsory hours of work, no performance standards and provides a warm room and subsidised meals to a bunch of self-opinionated windbags and busybodies."
>
> This remark not only shows that the British do not take their politicians too seriously, but also reflects some popular misunderstandings of parliament's role in the political system. Many people do not, for example, see their MPs doing the job they have been elected to perform and to an extent they are right: practice does not conform with theory. – *Is Democracy Working?* Ed. Sheila Browne (Newcastle: Tyne Tees Television, 1986), pp. 5-7.

The theory which underlies our political system could be summed up in the word "representation". At general elections each constituency of 60-65,000 voters chooses someone to represent it in the House of Commons.

There he – and it normally is a "he" – joins 651 other MPs elected by a total of 42.7 million voters. This body has the ultimate responsibility for governing the country until the next election.

At the next election our MP has to line up with other candidates once again and convince the voters in his constituency that his record is such that he deserves to be sent back to Westminster to carry on the good work. Does he listen? In theory, he ought to. Because if he does not, and behaves contrary to our wishes, then we can vote him out on election day: on that occasion he is again made accountable to us.

The system is seductively simple and clear. It places the House of Commons [...] at the centre of everything. A majority vote from this body, endorsed by the House of Lords and the Queen, determines the law of the land. In theory it can do anything it likes: reverse the decisions of previous parliaments, make legal past illegalities, even legislate that black is white if it so chooses. This "sovereign power" is our guarantee that nothing will overrule the will of our elected representatives.

This is the theory. The reality of government is more complicated however and the accountability of our representatives more tenuous.

The simple theory of representation explained above is modified in practice by a number of factors.

The Electoral System

1. General elections are infrequent – we have had only thirteen since 1945. Do politicians need to listen between elections – or just before them to make sure their story is right?

2. Some votes are "wasted" in that they are cast for candidates who are not elected. Two-thirds of all seats are regarded as "safe" for either Labour of Conservative; votes cast for other parties in these constituencies are unlikely to determine the outcome.

3. Our voting system provides imperfect representation. Our "first past the post" system rewards the big parties disproportionately and penalises small parties with thin national support. Thus, in 1983 the Conservatives were able to win 61% of the seats on 42.5% of the vote and the Alliance [of Liberals and Social Democrats] only 3.5% of the seats on 26% of the votes cast.

The House of Lords

It is sometimes easy to forget that the House of Lords still performs an important function in our political system. Since 1949 it has only had the power to delay decisions passed by the House of Commons for a maximum period of one year. However, all legislation must be discussed and passed by the Lords, too, and their Lordships' power of revision and amendment can often frustrate what the majority party in the House of Commons seeks to do. [...] It could be the case, therefore, that the decisions we wish our elected representatives to make are amended or reversed by a chamber comprising 1200 or so non-elected people (800 hereditary peers, 340 life peers, 26 bishops, 9 Law Lords).

The House of Lords

Party

According to theory MPs make judgments on their own, as individuals. In practice, however, they are all members of political parties. People do not vote for individuals normally, but for the parties they represent. Unless MPs toe the party line in Parliament they risk losing this essential electoral asset. It is hardly surprising, therefore, that they rarely deviate from the party line and that all but a few of the votes taken at the end of debates in the Commons can be predicted beforehand. With good discipline the majority party can stay in power for up to five years and there is little the opposition parties can do about it. Lord Hailsham has likened this to an "elective dictatorship"; in other words, once it has a majority, a political party can use the sovereign power of Parliament to do virtually what it likes until the next election comes round.

The Prime Minister

As the leader of the majority party the Prime Minister has immense power. If they want to advance their political careers, members of the governing party have to make themselves agreeable to the occupant of No. 10 Downing Street. Failure to do so might lead to dismissal from office or years of frustration on the backbenches.

The Cabinet Room

> **P**arliament will train you to talk; and above all things to hear with patience, unlimited quantities of foolish talk. – *Thomas Carlyle*

The Civil Service

Since the turn of the century the volume of legislation has expanded over thirty times and the size of the civil service over 15 times to its present total of 630,000. Some people argue that it has now become so vast and specialised that few ministers can understand the work of civil servants or control them effectively. Others go on to argue that senior civil servants use their experience, expertise and guile to outwit their political masters. If ministers, appointed by the majority party of the chamber which is supposed to represent us, cannot be relied on to control their departments then the whole edifice of elections and Parliament is called into question.

Pressure Groups

There are literally thousands of organisations seeking to influence specific areas of policy. The most important and powerful are those connected with business and trade unions; others seek to advance the interests of particular groups of people whilst others promote ideas and causes. New policies and legislation are often produced by ministers and civil servants in close consultation with pressure groups. [...] Certain MPs, moreover, accept fees for advancing the causes of specific pressure groups.

As government has become more complicated and extensive the role of the House of Commons has diminished in importance but it still performs several vital functions in the complex web of government.

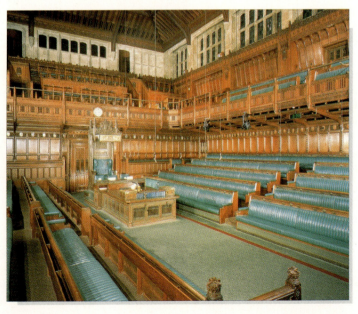

The House of Commons

Politics in Britain

6 Jonathan Lynn and Antony Jay
"The Smokescreen"

This extract from the BBC TV series *Yes Prime Minister* is a satire on the relationship between the government and the civil service – the bureaucracy which puts government policies into practice. In this episode the prime minister, Jim Hacker, wishes to reduce taxes. He is opposed by his senior civil servant, Sir Humphrey Appleby, who sees a reduction in taxation as a reduction in the influence of the civil service. The conflict is carried out with all the cunning one would expect of two clever political operators. – Jonathan Lynn and Antony Jay, *Yes Prime Minister* (London: BBC Books, 1989), pp. 190-196.

May 3rd

Humphrey and I had a meeting about a study paper that he had sent me on the subject of cancelling Trident and reintroducing conscription. It was very long, very fat and completely unreadable.

I showed it to him. He was pleased with it. "Ah yes, we can't get enough papers on that," he remarked smugly. "We need lots of input. We don't want to make any announcements until we have examined every implication and ramification." Familiar delaying tactics.

"This *is* going to happen, Humphrey," I told him firmly.

"Oh yes, Prime Minister." By *yes* he meant *no*. "Indeed it is, beyond question, at the appropriate juncture, in due course, in the fullness of time."

"No Humphrey," I replied sharply. "This century. This Parliament, in fact."

He shook his head sadly. "This Parliament? The time may not be ripe. It could turn out to be a banana skin."

Perhaps his doubts are a reflection of the curious obstinacy I am encountering from Eric (the Chancellor of the Exchequer). The paper shows that if my plan goes ahead we'll have one and a half billion pounds available for tax cuts. And the Chancellor, of all people opposes it. How can he oppose such a chance to win popularity from the voters? The only possibility, according to Humphrey, is that Eric is being advised by the Treasury, which apparently doesn't believe in giving money back.

This is always hard for a non-Treasury man to understand. I explained that the money is not the Treasury's, it is the taxpayers'.

"That is one view," Humphrey acknowledged. "But it is not the view the Treasury takes. Not once they have got their hands on it."

"But if they don't need the money ..." I began.

He interrupted me, puzzled. "I'm sorry?" he asked.

"If they don't need it ..." I reiterated, and was again stopped in mid-sentence.

"Taxation," said Humphrey loftily, "isn't about what

From left to right: Bernard Woolley, the prime minister's principal private secretary, Sir Humphrey Appleby, senior civil servant, Jim Hacker, prime minister

you need. The Treasury does not work out what it needs and then think how to raise the money. The Treasury pitches for as much as it can get away with and then thinks how to spend it. If the government started to give money back just because we didn't need it, we would be breaking with centuries of tradition. What would happen to the British Navy, for instance?"

I couldn't see any relevance to the question. "It would still be there. We still need a Navy."

Humphrey explained that, as we only have four capital ships, we only would *need* four Admirals and one Admiral of the Fleet. Whereas we have a total of sixty Admirals. And tempting though it would be to do away with fifty-six of them, the effect would be to reduce the number of serving officers all the way down, until there was hardly anybody left in the Navy at all. [...]

May 10th

Today I saw the way to get my tax cuts. And the help is going to come from a most unlikely source: the Minister of State for Health. Not only is he an unlikely source of help, he doesn't even know that he's going to help. And I'm certainly not going to tell him!

This is how it happened. Dr Thorn came to see me. He had sent me a paper on cigarettes, apparently, and the power and influence of the tobacco lobby in this country. [...] His idea was for the government to take action to eliminate smoking. He had a five-point plan:

1. A complete ban on all cigarette sponsorship.
2. A complete ban on all cigarette advertising, even at the point of sale.
3. Fifty million pounds to be spent on anti-smoking publicity.
4. A ban on smoking in all public places.
5. Progressive deterrent tax rises over five years until a packet of twenty costs about the same as a bottle of whisky.

It is a drastic scheme. He claims it should reduce smoking by at least eighty per cent. Even ninety per cent, perhaps. He reckons it will drive the tobacco companies out of business.

I had no immediate answer for such radical proposals. Of course it would have helped if I'd read his paper before the meeting, but one can't find time for everything! But he was very serious and I had to keep him happy. So I told him that obviously I agreed with him, basically, that smoking ought to be stopped. No question. And I told him that we would definitely stop it in due course, at the appropriate juncture, in the fullness of time. I could see Bernard nodding with approval in the background. I'm getting very good at Civil Service stalling techniques.

Dr Thorn could see what I was doing, though. "You mean, forget it?"

I assured him that that wasn't what I meant. And it wasn't! Well, not exactly! But we do have to be realistic. [...]

And then my *brilliant* idea occurred to me! A way to beat the Treasury. With Dr Peter Thorn's help, but without his knowledge. And not on the issue of smoking, but as a means of securing the tax cuts that I want.

I was very careful. I didn't *exactly* tell Thorn that I'd support him. But I told him he'd made his case, and that we could give his plan a try. I told him I'd even read his paper. I added 'again' just in time. [...]

I instructed Bernard to check that Peter Thorn's anti-smoking speeches are printed and distributed, and to make sure that everyone knows. It is particularly important that the Treasury gets to hear of it all soon.

Bernard, of course, had no idea of my plan and asked me if I thought I could possibly win this fight.

I smiled cheerfully. "Some you win, Bernard, and some you lose. This one I shall definitely lose."

Now he was completely baffled. "Then why ...?"

I saved my breath for him. "Because *when* I lose they'll have to give me something in return. If you were the Treasury, which would you rather give up – one and a half billion pounds of income tax revenue or four billion pounds of tobacco tax revenue?"

He smiled. "I'd prefer the income tax cut."

I nodded. "And that, as you know, is what I've wanted all along."

His face was full of admiration and respect. "So you're using cigarettes to create a sort of smokescreen?"

"Precisely," I said.

May 11th

Humphrey came to see me this morning. He was very tense. Clearly Bernard has been doing an excellent job of making sure that everyone knows about Dr Thorn's new policies.

"Prime Minister," he began, "I just wondered ... did you have an interesting chat with Dr Thorn?"

"Yes. He has proposed the elimination of smoking."

Sir Humphrey laughed derisively. "And how, pray, does he intend to achieve this? A campaign of mass hypnosis, perhaps?"

I remained calm. I leaned back in my chair and smiled confidently at him. "No. By raising taxes on tobacco sky high, and simultaneously prohibiting all cigarette advertising at the point of sale."

Humphrey chuckled confidently, but said nothing.

"Don't you think, " I asked, "that his position is admirably moral?"

He was as superior as only Humphrey can be. "Moral perhaps, but extremely silly. No one in their right mind could seriously contemplate such a proposal."

"I'm contemplating it," I said.

"Yes, of *course*," he replied without a moment's hesitation, the patronising smile wiped instantly from his face. "Don't misunderstand me, of course it's right to contemplate all proposals that come from your government, but no sane man could ever *support* it."

"I'm supporting it," I said.

"And quite right too, Prime Minister, if I may say so." His footwork is so fast that one might be forgiven for not noticing he totally reversed his opinion with each sentence he uttered.

I gave him the chance to come over to my side. "So you'll support it?" I asked.

"Support it?" He was emphatic. "I support it wholeheartedly! A splendid, novel, romantic, well-meaning, imaginative, do-gooding notion."

As I thought. He is totally against it!

"The only problem is," he continued, "that there are powerful arguments against such a policy."

"And powerful arguments for it," I replied.

"Oh, *absolutely*! But *against* it," he persisted, "there are those who would point out that the tax on tobacco is a major source of revenue to the government."

"But there are also those who would point out that tobacco is a major cause of death from a number of killer diseases."

Humphrey nodded earnestly. "Yes. Indeed. Shocking. If it's true. But of course, no *definite* causal link has ever been proved, has it?"

"The statistics are unarguable," I said. He looked amused. "Statistics? You can prove anything with statistics." "Even the truth," I remarked.

"Ye-es," he acknowledged with some reluctance. "£4 billion revenue per annum is a considerable sum. They would say," he added hastily, for fear of being thought he was taking sides in this dispute. *They* were clearly the Treasury.

I remarked that a hundred thousand unnecessary deaths a year – minimum – is a hideous epidemic. He agreed that it was appalling. So I went for the kill. "It costs the

> **G**od bless the civil service
> The nation's saving grace.
> While we're expecting democracy
> They're laughing in our face. — Billy Bragg

NHS a fortune to deal with the victims. So the Treasury would be delighted if we discouraged it."

This was a tactical error. Sir Humphrey swung confidently on to the offensive. "Now I think you're wrong there, Prime Minister."

I couldn't see how I could be wrong. "Smoking-related diseases," I said, referring to Dr Thorn's paper which I had in front of me, "cost the NHS £165 million a year."

But Sir Humphrey had been well briefed too, by the Treasury and by their friends in the tobacco lobby. "We have gone into that," he replied. "It's been shown that, if these extra 100,000 people a year had lived to a ripe old age, they would have cost us even more in pensions and social security than they did in medical treatment. So, financially, it is unquestionably better that they continue to die at about the present rate."

I was shocked. I've been in politics a long time and not much shocks me any more. But his cynicism is truly appalling. [...]

"Humphrey," I said, "when cholera killed 30,000 people in 1833 we got the Public Health Act. When smog killed 2,500 people in 1952 we got the Clean Air Act. When a commercial drug kills fifty or sixty people we get it withdrawn from sale, even if it's doing lots of good to many patients. But cigarettes kill 100,000 people a year and what do we get?"

"Four billion pounds a year," he replied promptly. "Plus about 25,000 jobs in the tobacco industry, a flourishing cigarette export business which helps the balance of trade. Also, 250,000 jobs indirectly related to tobacco – newsagents, packing, transport ..."

I interrupted. "These figures are just guesses."

"No," he said, "they are government statistics." He saw me smile, and hurriedly continued: "That is to say, they are facts."

I couldn't resist it. "You mean, your statistics are facts, but my facts are just statistics."

7 The Story of the Tolpuddle Martyrs

The Tolpuddle Martyrs were not the founders of British trade unionism nor were they the first trade unionists to be transported, but their struggles and sacrifices were an inspiration to later trade unionists. In 1834 six agricultural labourers from the village of Tolpuddle in southwest England were sentenced to transportation to Australia for seven years. Why? The law said it was because they had taken an oath which was illegal under the Mutiny Act of 1797. But history shows there was more to it than that. – *The Story of the Tolpuddle Martyrs* (London: Trades Union Congress, 3rd. ed., 1991), pp. 1-10.

Skeleton at the plough

Wages in the 1830s

The lot of the agricultural labourer in the 1830s was not an enviable one. In Tolpuddle, the labourer's wage in 1830 was nine shillings a week. In succeeding years it was reduced to eight shillings then seven. In 1834 the farm labourers were threatened with a further reduction to six shillings a week.

At this time in Tolpuddle there was a man of outstanding character, George Loveless, and under his leadership some of the men considered together how they might defend themselves against these progressive reductions of their wages. They tried to come to terms with their employers, using the Vicar of Tolpuddle as an intermediary. Promises were made, but were not kept.

A Union is Formed

The Tolpuddle men turned for advice to the Grand Consolidated Trades Union, which was led by Robert Owen and which was then quickly winning members in industrial centres up and down the country. Two delegates of the Union came to Tolpuddle and as a result the Friendly Society of Agricultural Labourers was formed by the men.

The men form a union.

Politics in Britain

Legal Repression Follows

At the eruption of trade unionism in the village, the employers and the local magistrates took fright. Were they to be faced with the riots and rick burning which had taken place in 1830? One of the magistrates, James Frampton, sought guidance from the Home Secretary, Lord Melbourne. The upshot was that George Loveless and five of his fellow labourers were arrested on 24 February 1834, imprisoned in Dorchester, and at the Dorchester Assizes in March 1834, were sentenced to seven years' transportation to Australia.

The Law's Excuse

There can be no doubt that the 'crime' for which the men were punished was that of organising themselves and others in a trade union. But in law some other offence had to be found, for since an Act of 1824 trade unions had no longer been illegal in themselves.

Many of the trade unions of this time, still fearing legal repression and retaliation by employers, required members to take oaths of loyalty to the union and of secrecy as to its affairs. This procedure was common practice in other organisations, such as the Freemasons and the Orangemen's Lodges. It was adopted by the Tolpuddle union and advantage was taken of this fact to charge the men under the Mutiny Act of 1797. This Act had been passed to deal with a mutiny in the Navy and forbade the taking of 'unlawful oaths'. It was impossible since 1824 to charge the men directly with the organisation of a union, which was no longer a crime. But the oath procedure of the union laid them open to a charge under the 1797 Act.

On 22 February the six men were arrested. They were:
George Loveless
James Loveless (George's brother)
James Hammett
Thomas Standfield
John Standfield (Thomas's son)
James Brine.

Trial and Sentence

Following their arrest, the six men were lodged in Dorchester jail. They were tried in the Crown Court on 17 March 1834, and two days later, sentence of seven years' transportation – the maximum sentence – was passed. [...]

Before passing sentence the judge asked if the defendants had anything to say. Thereupon, George Loveless handed him a paper on which he had written:

My Lord, if we had violated any law,
it was not done intentionally;
we have injured no man's reputation, character, person or property;
we were uniting together to preserve ourselves,
our wives and our children, from utter degradation and starvation.
We challenge any man, or number of men, to prove that we have acted,
or intended to act, different from the above statement.

In passing sentence, the judge said:

The object of all legal punishment is not altogether with a view of operating on the offenders themselves, it is also for the sake of offering an example and warning [...]

Following their sentence, five of the men were sent to the hulks at Portsmouth, and in April 1834 set sail in the convict ship, Surrey, for New South Wales where they landed in August. George Loveless, who after the trial was ill in Dorchester prison, sailed in the William Metcalf convict ship in May 1834, and landed in Tasmania in September. [...] The men had hard and harrowing experiences overseas. They worked in chain gangs, in penal settlements and on farms where their status was, if any, little more than that of serfs.

James Brine, aged 25

Thomas Standfield, aged 51

John Standfield, aged 25

George Loveless, aged 41

James Loveless, aged 29

Hammett said he was:

sold like a slave for £1.

The convicts' names were written on slips of paper, the agents drew lots, each man at £1 per head.

The Great Agitation

Meanwhile, at home much was happening in the cause of the six men and their families. On 24 March 1834, there was a Grand Meeting of the Working Classes, called by the Grand National Consolidated Trade Union on the instigation of Robert Owen. The chairman was Dr Arthur S. Wade, the vicar of St Nicholas, Warwick. He was a leading figure in London Radicalism. This meeting was attended by over 10,000 people; it was but the beginning. The agitation spread and grew. The London Central Dorchester Committee was formed, and in addition to carrying on the campaign for the men's pardon, saw to the welfare of their dependants by means of funds raised by public subscription.

A vast demonstration took place in April 1834. More than 30,000 people assembled in Copenhagen Fields near to where King's Cross station now stands. Fearing disorder, the government had troops at hand and 5,000 special constables had been sworn in. But the whole demonstration was carried through with discipline and decorum. A procession was led to Whitehall by Owen and Wade, with a petition to the Home Secretary carried by twelve men. Melbourne, however, refused to accept the petition, saying that if it was presented on another day and in a more becoming manner he would lay it before the King.

The agitation for the men's release was steadily maintained. William Cobbett, Joseph Hume, Thomas Wakley and other MPs kept the question constantly before Parliament. Petitions came from all over the country. Hume announced in the Commons that over 800,000 people had signed them.

The demonstration against the transportation of the Martyrs, Copenhagen Fields, London, 21 April, 1834

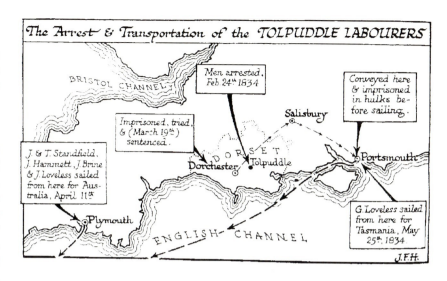

In June 1835, Lord John Russell (who had now become Home Secretary) proposed a conditional pardon for the six men. While all would be pardoned, Hammett, Brine and the two Standfields would be required to remain in the colony until they had been there two years. George and James Loveless, regarded as ringleaders, would not even be allowed to return.

Those who had spoken for the men were not satisfied and the agitation continued. In February 1836, Lord John Russell amended his previous offer by proposing that George and James Loveless should be allowed to return after three years in the colonies – but that was still not good enough. Under further pressure, Russell agreed on 14 March 1836 that all the men should have a full and free pardon.

8. "Should We Ban Strikes in Key Public Services?"

Politics in Britain

In the summer of 1994 railway and signal workers started a long series of strikes to support their wage claim. These strikes caused widespread disruption and renewed discussion about how far strikes in important public services should be allowed. The issue was debated on Channel 4 TV and in *The Observer*, 28 August 1994, p. 18.

FOR

Ira Chalphin, *Institute of Directors*

This country is dealing with its third national rail strike in five years. Such a poor record is bad for the railways and the country. We should not allow the economy to be held hostage because of an outdated system of settling industrial disputes in essential services.

Many other industrialised countries have special procedures for dealing with disputes in key industries. Britain is an exception. Workers on strike in rail, water or electricity companies have the same legal immunities as do workers in, for example, a supermarket. The key difference is that consumers can shop elsewhere. In essential services, there are few if any alternatives.

What should be done? First, Parliament should impose a statutory duty to supply certain services such as gas, water, electricity, telecommunications, health and emergency services. Second, the legislation should impose an obligation to provide compensation to customers when the obligation is not fulfilled.

Third, there should be a new tort of organising industrial action in selected essential services. Existing workers should receive a one-off compensation payment for a unilateral change to contracts of employment.

This would encourage 'no-strike' deals, providing for binding arbitration as a last-resort option.

Certain services necessary for the maintenance of public health and safety and fundamental to continuous economic activity need to be protected against disruption. Britain's strike record has improved substantially over the past 15 years, but problems remain. Now is the time to complete the unfinished business of trade union reform.

AGAINST

Roger Poole, *of the health and local government union, Unison*

Threats to outlaw strikes in essential services have become a familiar feature of high-profile disputes in the public sector since 1979. For those of us who value living in a democracy, the idea represents a sinister shift towards outlawing all industrial action.

This government has backed off from implementing outline legislation on the stocks. Its will to shackle public sector unions has never been wanting, but the stumbling blocks have been the practical application and complexities of legislation. These include identifying which services are essential to the smooth running of the country.

Should the definition cover only the emergency services – fire, police and ambulance? Or should it encompass health, transport, energy, water, electricity, telecommunications, schools and prisons? Should local government and the civil service be included?

The privatisation of gas, water and electricity compounds the problem, pushing the scope of potential legislation beyond the public sector. There would also be difficulties with enforcing sanctions. Would we seriously contemplate jailing 'offenders'?

Instead of contemplating ways of lessening the impact of disruption, the Government should concentrate on eradicating the causes of discontent – poverty, exploitation, inequality and unfairness.

The Government must not be allowed to remove any more of our democratic rights. We should rather concentrate on how we can strengthen our democracy. A free and strong trade union movement is an essential prerequisite to a civilised and democratic society.

VIEWS

Eric Hammond, *retired general secretary of EEPTU, who negotiated a no-strike agreement in 1988*

We got a lot of stick for our no-strike agreement but we were misunderstood. I believe workers should voluntarily give up their rights to strike; it can't be imposed on them. With the last series of strikes by the ambulance men, I wrote to Margaret Thatcher saying the men had a case, but what they were doing was bad for the public. We began quite a correspondence.

Jarvis Cocker, *lead singer of Pulp*

My girlfriend works in mental health. People who go into nursing care about others, and that's played upon by the papers, who say "oh, people might die if you strike". It's emotional blackmail. I'm with the signalmen every inch of the way. People should be glad of having a day off – you shouldn't live for work. You can roll in at 11 and say I had a terrible time getting here.

Ian Lowes, *convenor of GMB on Liverpool Council, who led the 1979 cremation staff and gravediggers' strike*

The strike of 1979 was horrendous. Death is the most emotional issue and relatives don't think rationally. Our workers were being threatened, but there were workers whose own relatives had died and were waiting to be buried. You don't enter into a strike like that lightly. But we had to draw attention to the conditions we were working under which weren't being recognised by the employers. We defend the right to strike, but in 1991, when a load of redundancies were made, we didn't use it. We were bearing in mind the need to win public support.

Harry Greenway, *Tory MP*

I respect the right to withdraw labour. However, I believe the police and armed forces should not have the right to strike, and nor should MPs. MPs are often absolutely crucial to the lives of their constituents. There are deaths in the family, which are deeply distressing, which people need help with.

Tess Gill, *barrister specialising in employment law*

Of course not – this is a fundamental human right. What would happen to all the auxiliary workers in hospitals, the cleaners, who are so badly paid? Other countries function perfectly well without a ban.

Staff of British Telecom demonstrate in London for better pay.

"You're not happy here, are you?"

Tony Benn, *Labour MP*

The banning of strikes in the essential public services was first advocated by Mussolini in Fascist Italy. If it is done, it introduces industrial conscription – work is no longer voluntary, but compulsory. Multi-national companies which own plants can close them down at any time, without any restraints at all, but labour is already tightly controlled. It's part of the imbalance between the rights of capital and the rights of labour.

Gerald Hartup, *the Freedom Association, a right-wing pressure group*

We accept the right of essential public workers to strike except when it is contrary to public safety. We also maintain that the employer has the right to replace labour at the end of the day, and in some cases has a responsibility to do so. The signalmen are putting people out of work and children, as a result, may go hungry. Another effect is that stations become marginalised, communities are isolated, and consequently there are tragedies.

Politics in Britain

9 Political Advertising*

Political advertising is an important element of election campaigning even though most political scientists doubt whether either the campaigns or the advertising influence many voters. What advertising does seem to do is strengthen certain trends and attitudes which already exist in society. – Saatchi and Saatchi Advertising, 80 Charlotte Street, London W1A 1AQ (Conservative Party advertisement). – The Labour Party, 150 Walworth Road, London SE17 1JT (Labour Party advertisement).

IN COME LABOUR.

In an effort to get into power, Labour has made billions of pounds worth of promises. But they haven't told you where the money is coming from. Because they suspect you won't like the answer. See below.

INCOME TAXES.

£10,000	SECRETARY Single	£796 MORE under Labour	£20,000	TEACHER Married, 2 children, mortgage.	£1272 MORE under Labour
£14,000	NURSE Single	£1296 MORE under Labour	£24,000	ENGINEER Married, 2 children, mortgage.	£2037 MORE under Labour
£17,500	ELECTRICIAN Married, 2 children, mortgage.	£960 MORE under Labour	£25,000	JOURNALIST Married with mortgage	£2379 MORE under Labour

It's obvious to everyone but Labour – high taxes would destroy incentive and cripple recovery. Conservatives want taxes as low as possible to put more money in people's pockets, create more demand and more jobs.

CONSERVATIVE [X]

An advertisement for the Conservative Party

Politics in Britain

> **D**emocracy consists of choosing our dictators, after they've told you what they think you think you want to hear. — *Alan Coren*

> **C**onservative, n.: a statesman who is enamoured of existing evils, as distinguished from the Liberal who wishes to replace them with others. — *Ambrose Bierce*

PAGE 8   DAILY MIRROR, Wednesday, March 11, 1992   ADVERTISEMENT

Georgina Norris died because the NHS is short of money.

Meanwhile, the Tories are cutting taxes to keep their election hopes alive.

Georgina Norris was born with a serious heart condition.

She had Fallot's tetralogy, which affects one in 1,000 babies.

But surgeons can correct the problem. The operation has a success rate of better than 70%.

Doctors at Great Ormond Street planned to operate on October 29 last year. But the day before Georgina was due to be admitted, the operation was cancelled.

The hospital has nine beds in its general intensive care unit, but the doctors are only given enough money to run five.

And Georgina's bed in the cardiac intensive care unit had been taken over at the last minute by an emergency.

To her parent's relief, she was taken into hospital on Sunday November 10 for an operation the following Tuesday.

The next day, she was sent home. Two emergencies had been admitted the night before and doctors had to tell her parents that cardiac intensive care was full.

A third date was fixed, December 11.

But on Friday November 15, four days after she'd been sent home, she collapsed unconscious after her heart stopped beating.

She was put on a ventilator and rushed to Great Ormond Street.

This time, she was an emergency. This time, they operated.

But this time, it was too late.

For the next 36 hours, Georgina's parents sat at her bedside, watching her life slip away.

She would never regain consciousness.

At 12.05 am on Sunday, November 17 1991, Georgina Norris died.

She was eighteen months old.

Today, the day after Norman Lamont decided to spend money on tax cuts, there are still four empty beds in the general intensive care unit at Great Ormond Street.

Labour

An advertisement for the Labour Party

10 "Portrait of the Electorate"

The table shows in percentages how different social groups voted at two general elections. By studying it we may find some of the factors which influence the way people vote and see trends in voting behaviour. – *The Sunday Times*, 12 April 1992, p. 2.6.

1992 voters		1987 vote Con	Lab	L/D	1992 vote Con	Lab	L/D
100	Total	43	32	23	43	35	18
49	Men	43	32	23	41	37	18
51	Women	43	32	23	44	34	18
14	18-24	33	40	21	35	39	19
19	25-34	39	33	25	40	38	18
33	35-54	45	29	24	43	34	19
34	54+	46	31	21	46	34	17
23	Pensioner	47	31	21	48	34	16
19	AB-prof	57	14	26	56	20	22
24	C1-white collar	51	21	26	52	25	19
27	C2-skilled	40	36	22	38	41	17
30	DE-semi- and unskilled	30	48	20	30	50	15
67	Owner occupier	50	23	25	49	30	19
23	Council tenant	22	56	19	24	55	15
7	Private tenant	39	37	21	33	40	21
7	Men 18-24	42	37	19	39	35	18
7	Women 18-24	31	42	24	30	43	19
9	Men 25-34	41	33	24	40	37	17
10	Women 25-34	37	33	27	40	38	18
16	Men 35-54	42	32	24	40	37	19
17	Women 35-54	47	27	25	46	32	19
17	Men 55+	45	31	23	43	38	17
17	Women 55+	46	32	20	49	32	17
9	Men 65+	47	30	22	44	38	16
9	Women 65+	46	33	20	51	31	17
4	Unemployed (m)	21	56	20	24	52	17
3	Unemployed (f)	23	54	19	26	51	16
17	North (m)	34	42	20	33	46	14
19	North (f)	33	41	22	36	43	15
13	Midland (m)	46	34	19	44	38	16
13	Midland (f)	45	29	24	46	36	16
19	South (m)	49	22	28	46	29	22
20	South (f)	51	24	24	50	27	22
	Homeowners:						
36	Middle-class	57	15	26	56	21	20
31	Working-class	43	32	23	41	39	17
	Council tenants:						
2	Middle-class	28	41	24	34	40	18
21	Working-class	21	58	18	22	58	15
	Trade unions:						
23	Members	30	42	26	30	47	19
15	Men	31	42	25	30	48	18
8	Women	29	41	27	31	44	21

Politics in Britain

The British class system

"Which party's distortions, evasions and outright lies do you prefer?"

"If my opinion were to be polled next week, what would it be?"

11 | "Electoral Reform: Which System Is Best?"*

This article from the *Guardian* discusses some of the ways in which votes at the ballot box are translated into seats in parliament. Britain's first past the post system seems particularly unfair since in the 1992 general election it allowed the Conservative Party to win over 50% of the seats in parliament with only 43% of the votes. The Liberal Democrats, on the other hand, gained only 3% of the seats after obtaining 17% of the votes. – *The Guardian*, 8 April 1992, p. 4.

Electoral reform is on the agenda in several European countries as well as in Britain. The rise of fringe extremists in the French, German and Italian elections has made consensus rule by middle-ground parties more difficult as their ability to obtain overall majorities is reduced.

Almost all European countries use some form of proportional representation. But now, some European politicians are looking wistfully at Britain's first-past-the-post system. Others say that a reform of PR is needed.

PR aims to produce a distribution of seats among parties and individuals that reflects the percentage of votes cast in their favour.

The following are the main forms of PR used in Europe:

– **The Single Transferable Vote**, as practised in Ireland and Malta, is favoured by the Liberal Democrats. In Ireland, constituencies elect up to five MPs. Voters indicate their order of preference for candidates. If a candidate has more votes than the quota needed to win a seat, the surplus is distributed to other candidates as indicated by the preference.

– **The Additional Member System**, used by Germany, elects some candidates through constituencies as in first-past-the-post elections and others according to an overall voting trend. Parties must win at least 5 per cent of the vote to qualify for seats, a hurdle meant to keep extremist parties out.

– **A List System**. This is a purer form of proportional representation in which parties put forward lists of candidates according to the strength of party support. The list method forms the basis of electoral systems in Sweden, Italy, Belgium and Spain.

Politics in Britain

– **The Alternative Vote** is the system used to select Australia's lower house. Electors choose a first preference candidate in a single member constituency who must gain half the vote to win. If not, the second preference votes are shared out and so on until a majority winner emerges.

– **Reinforced Proportional Representation**, used in Greece, reserves a bloc of about 20 seats for the party which comes first. Greece experimented with a more proportional method in 1989 but abandoned it after two unstable governments were elected.

> **D**emocracy is a process by which the people are free to choose who gets the blame. – *Laurence J. Peters*

"Election Results"*

The present British electoral system and some of its alternatives showing the results they produced and would have produced at the general election on 9 April 1992. The figures are taken from *The Independent on Sunday*, 12 April 1992, p. 20.

	The result under the first past the post system on 9 April 1992			The result as it would have been under the					
				alternative vote system		single transferable system		additional member system	
	% of total votes	seats	% of seats	seats	% of seats	seats	% of seats	seats	% of seats
Conservative	43.0	336	51.6	323	49.6	275	42.2	346	45.9
Labour	35.4	271	41.6	261	40.1	237	36.4	283	37.7
Liberal Democrats	17.7	20	3.1	39	6.0	102	15.7	89	11.9
Scottish National Party	2.1	3	0.5	6	0.9	17	2.6	10	1.3
Plaid Cymru	0.4	4	0.6	5	0.8	3	0.5	4	0.5
Ulster Parties	2.2	17	2.6	17	2.6	17	2.6	19	2.5

John Major, leader of the Conservative Party is playing tennis with Neil Kinnock, leader of the Labour Party at the time of the 1992 election, and Paddy Ashdown, leader of the Liberal Democrats. This cartoon appeared on 14 April 1992 in the *Guardian*.

Politics in Britain

12 An Interview with John Major:
What do the Conservatives Stand for?*

Politicians of all parties in all democratic countries make promises, work out policies and use slogans in an attempt to gain people's votes. In this interview the BBC reporter and commentator James Naughtie questions the British prime minister, John Major, about some of his promises, policies and slogans. Besides dealing with a number of general political topics – the economy, the welfare state, society's values, and education – this interview shows us some of the ways in which John Major attempts to answer the criticisms implied in the questions. – John Major, "The World This Weekend", Interview on BBC Radio 4, London, 2 January 1994.

John Major became prime minister in 1990

James Naughtie: But you see on the question of confidence in government this all ties in with your theme of the moment: back to basics, values, and so on. Now, you're stressing self-responsibility as one of the elements in that. And people wonder what it means. Does it mean, for example, that they should be preparing to pay for more of their education, more of their health care, more of their pension arrangements, than has traditionally been the case?

John Major: Many people have raised all sorts of artificial fears about the welfare state. I'm in the business of sustaining the welfare state, not destroying the welfare state. But that means it has to be put in a position where it can be sustained. And that is essentially what we're doing. That's true of the health reforms which are becoming increasingly entrenched and I believe successful year after year. And it's true also of the necessary social security changes that we have made. Over the past decade or more expenditure on social security has risen, year in year out, good years, bad years, years of boom, years of no growth at all, by around 3% over and above the rate of growth. Now that isn't sustainable over the long term. In fact if nobody acted to deal with that problem, the day would come when suddenly there would be a huge crisis. We're acting now to ensure that the welfare state is sustainable over the long term. And that is the right way for a government with long-term aims to behave.

[...]

James Naughtie: Now, when you talk about values, 'back to basics', do you accept that you're asking for something from people and they will want something from you? And they want to know that the government is above all dealing fairly and perhaps they need to know what'll become of the welfare state as we've been talking about in the last few minutes. And also whether the disparities in wealth that became clear in the eighties, are in your view, a natural part in the end of any healthy society?

John Major: Let me just add a little more about 'back to basics' before it gets too widely misunderstood. We are talking about values. And I mean values across the whole range of human activity. There are some certain lasting human values that are instinctive to the British. Everyone knows what they are: respect, courtesy, obedience to the law, self-discipline, no-nonsense distinctions between right and wrong. There's nothing particularly fresh or novel about those. They are known to everyone in the country and understood by them. But over so much of the last twenty or thirty years it seems to me that they've almost been pushed aside. They've been taken for granted, neglected, pushed to one side and not operated on. I don't want to overcomplicate what is simple but I think we need to place those instinctive values, which the British have long cared for and accepted, smack in the middle of our public life again. And by our public life I don't just mean people in public life, I mean life in the United Kingdom and that is what we're proposing to do.

James Naughtie: But one of the ways in which this has been interpreted by your ministers and by the people in public debate has been on this question of family values. Now do you accept that one of the biggest assaults on the cohesion of the family has been the economic difficulties that many people have suffered in the last ten or fifteen years, much of it under a Conservative government?

John Major: Well, if you take the last ten or fifteen years, I mean for most of the 1980s, there was very significant economic growth, and an improvement in living standards for families right across the country. I think you need to take a longer period. I think you need to take a thirty-year period to look at the change in the ways many of these values are themselves interpreted.

James Naughtie: But many people now have found themselves not benefiting from the things which benefited other people in the eighties. The gap has widened. We've seen today figures on the number of children who grow up in difficult circumstances. Now you ...

John Major: They're bogus figures. I mean with great respect they're bogus figures. This is taking as a poverty line the level of income support. But of course the value of income support has risen. Of course if the value of income support rises, more people have incomes below that level. [...]

We want to open up opportunity to everybody, wherever they come from. That's what I meant when I talked about a classless society, not sort of some grey conformity as some people interpreted it. When I talk about a classless society I'm talking about a society in which everybody, wherever they may come from, whatever they may start with, will have the same opportunities to progress as other people who perhaps start from quite different circumstances. That's exactly what we're seeking to do: the education reforms and with reforms right across the whole of government programme.

[...]

James Naughtie: Is it true that in education one of the ways that you see this being expressed is in a new emphasis in discipline?

John Major: I think one needs to be clear what one means about discipline. What I do not mean is harsh regimentation in schools. I emphatically do not mean that. Over the last twenty or thirty years schools have overwhelmingly become more friendly places than they were in the past. I thoroughly welcome that. And I wouldn't wish to lose that. What I am concerned about is reinforcing the authority of teachers and headteachers in particular in schools. I do think they need the authority to deal with bad behaviour. Many headteachers would argue these days that they have less authority than they themselves would wish. So I believe we do need to establish an orderly atmosphere in schools. I think there needs to be no doubt about what the school rules are. I personally, I know this is controversial with some people, I personally think it is attractive to have school uniforms for a range of reasons and I hope increasingly schools will move towards them.

[...] I personally favour homework. I personally, again this is controversial with some educationalists, very strongly favour team sport.

13 A Political Speech:
Tony Benn on Britain and Europe*

Tony Benn, Labour MP for the constituency of Chesterfield in Derbyshire, is among the most powerful public speakers inside and outside parliament. This is a transcript of part of a speech he made in the House of Commons on 20 November 1991 in which he criticised Britain's membership of the European Union and the signing of the Maastricht treaty. It is taken from the videocassette Tony Benn, *Speaking up in Parliament* (London: Silverglade Associates, 1993).

> **C**hurchill (when a cabbage was thrown at him while electioneering): "I asked for the man's ear, not his head."

[Tony Benn introduces his speech on the cassette:]
Britain's relations with the European Economic Community have divided all political parties for more than a generation and in 1991 at the time of the Maastricht summit, proposals were brought forward to convert the community to a full European Union. In the debate that occurred at that time it was an opportunity to present not nationalistic arguments against Maastricht but democratic arguments and in particular as far as I was concerned the right of the British people to give their consent explicitly to this major change before it came into effect. Today the European Union is in effect and this debate will continue for many years to come.

[The speech:]
There are three things that have interested me about this debate. First of all there is the fundamental agreement between the three party leaders. The prime minister is on the eve of negotiations. He has to be cautious. The leader of the opposition is hoping to take over. He can be bolder. The Liberal Party, far from office, can be quite clear about its objectives. But there isn't really any disagreement at all about what is happening, which is that we should move first from the original membership through the Single European Act into something stronger.

The second thing which interests me about this debate is the degree of caution that has emerged from people who, when we discussed it 20 years ago, were more uncritical about it. And the third thing. Perhaps I may be allowed to say with some satisfaction that 21 years after I urged a referendum I should have won over the Right Honourable lady, the member for Finchley, and the member for Yeovil to my cause. Even if you have to wait 21 years, it's worth waiting for some recognition that people have a right in their government.

I recognise when the three front benches are in agreement I'm in a minority. I accept that, and my next job is to explain to the people of Chesterfield what we have decided. And the first thing I have to explain to them is: my dear constituents, in future you will be governed by people you do not elect and cannot remove. I'm sorry about it. They may give you better creches, they might give you shorter working hours. But you can't remove them. Now the importance of democracy – I know it sounds negative but I've always thought it very positive – is that you can remove without bloodshed the people who govern you. You can get rid of a Callaghan, you can get rid of a Wilson. You can get rid of a Right Honourable lady – even by internal processes. You can get rid of a Huntingdon. But you can't do it in this structure. [...]

Secondly you're saying to the people – you know my favourite friends, the Chartists and the Suffragettes – that all your struggles to get control of the ballot were a waste of time. We're going to be run in future by a few

Tony Benn, Labour MP

white persons, like they did in 1832, and the instrument, I might add, is the royal prerogative of treaty making. For the first time since 1649 the Crown makes the laws. All right, advised by the prime minister.

You've got to ask yourself what will happen when people realise that that's what we've done. [...] If you lose the power to sack your government a number of things happen. First of all people just slope off and apathy could destroy democracy. When turnout drops below 50% you're in danger. Well, the United States – very low turnout. [...] The second thing you can do is riot. Riot is an old-fashioned method for drawing attention to what is wrong in the government. It's very difficult for an elected person ever to admit it, but riots in Strangeways produced some prison reforms. Riot has historically played a much larger part in British politics than we allow it to be known. The third thing is nationalism. Instead of blaming the Treaty of Rome you say it's those Germans again, the French. And you build nationalism out of frustration at the fact that you can't get your way through the ballot box. And with nationalism comes repression. [...]

> **O**nce when a British prime minister sneezed, men half a world away blew their noses. Now when a British prime minister sneezes nobody else will even say "bless you". – *Bernard Levin*

14 | "A Democratic Checklist"*

Every country claims to be democratic, but how democratic are they really? A panel of experts – academics, journalists and civil rights campaigners – have tried to judge how democratic every country in the world is. Each has been given a number of points out of a total of 100, and graded from 'highly democratic' to 'undemocratic'. Finland came top. The U.K. was level with Poland and just behind Benin. – *Bite the Ballot*, Supplement to the *New Statesman & Society,* 29 April 1994, p. 15.

Method

The panel were asked to judge the quality of democracy within a society as a whole, not just the government or state. [...]

In order to ensure consistency and minimise the inevitable element of subjectivity, we used a checklist of ten factors, adding a special weighting factor that has been used to take account of special factors like famine and war.

Politics in Britain

The Checklist

Voting
1. Is the head of state and/or government elected regularly through free and fair elections?
2. Is the legislature/parliament elected regularly through free and fair elections?

Participation
3. Is there a wide franchise, with real participation in the political process and a high turnout in elections, both local and national?
4. Is there an atmosphere where political questions are openly discussed? Is there an education system that encourages participation and citizenship?

Freedom
5. Are people free to organise in parties or other groups of their choice?
6. Is there freedom of expression? Are the media free to criticise the government? Is ownership of the media restricted? Do the media reflect and express a range of political views?
7. Is there an opposition with the opportunity to put its case to the people?

Rights
8. Are there rights for minorities – ethnic, religious and cultural? Do such minorities participate in the political process?
9. Is there an independent judiciary, and a rule of law that protects citizens from arbitrary arrest and torture?
10. Are there social and economic rights – of property, association, choice of residence, and the right to reasonable living standards – that facilitate political participation?

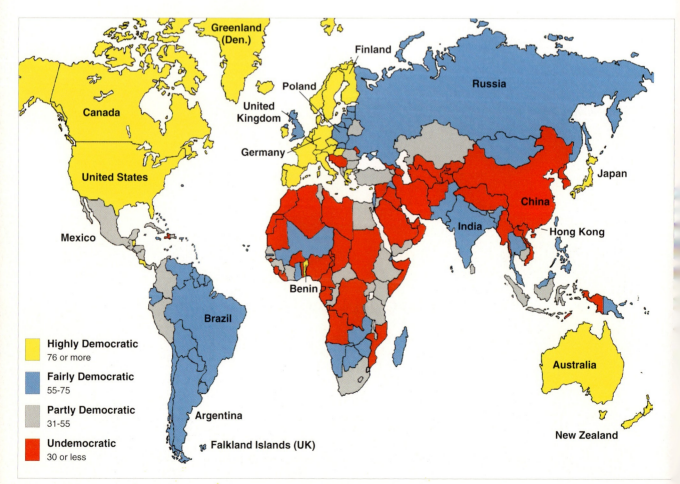

How democratic?

Study Aids

Abbreviations

n.	=	noun	esp.	=	especially
v.	=	verb	poet.	=	poetical(ly)
adj.	=	adjective	s.b.	=	somebody
adv.	=	adverb	s.o.	=	someone
part.	=	participle	s.th.	=	something
prep.	=	preposition	o.s.	=	oneself
conj.	=	conjunction	i.e.	=	that is
interj.	=	interjection	l.	=	line
sing.	=	singular	ll.	=	lines
pl.	=	plural	p.	=	page
BrE	=	British English	pp.	=	pages
AmE	=	American English	f.	=	and the following (page, line etc.)
intro	=	introduction	ff.	=	and the following (pages, lines etc.)
mod.	=	modern	e.g.	=	for example

Note:
Many British political offices and institutions can be spelt with either capital or lower case letters, e.g. prime minister/Prime Minister, parliament/Parliament, government/Government. Which is used depends on the author and on the publisher. In the texts we have kept the original spelling but in all the annotations we have used lower case letters. Other words can be spelt either with or without a hyphen, e.g. first past the post/first-past-the-post. Both are correct. In the case of poll tax four variants are possible and all are correct: poll tax, Poll Tax, poll-tax, Poll-Tax.

The phonetic transcriptions follow the *Longman Dictionary of Contemporary English (DCE)* and J. C. Wells, *Longman Pronunciation Dictionary*.

Politics in Britain

Title Page

Vocabulary

strife (n.): trouble between people, conflict - **unpalatable** (adj.): unpleasant and difficult for the mind to accept - **raving** (adj.): talking wildly as if mad - **loony** (adj.): extremely foolish - **to cast** (v.): to make (a vote) in an election

Explanations

general election: see p. 50 - **David 'Screaming Lord' Sutch**: (1940-): David Sutch started out as a pop singer in 1959. His trademark was to appear on stage in outrageous costumes, including aristocratic dress, hence his nickname 'Screaming Lord Sutch'. In 1981 David Sutch decided to form the Official Monster Raving Loony Party. He explained the name thus: Official - no other party in Britain has the word Official in its name, so all the other parties are unofficial; Monster - he had a monster act and there was nothing more monstrous than politicians; Raving - all politicians rave and he had been a raver for years; Loony - everybody had told him that he was a real loony to stand for parliament. While David Sutch and his Official Monster Raving Loony Party and the poster in particular have a satirical (see p. 28) intention, he can also be seen within a long tradition of English eccentrics, whose aim is to go in for extraordinary but harmless activities. The party has managed to obtain five seats on local councils. His story can be read in his autobiography *Life as Sutch* published by HarperCollins, 1991.

Picture

The picture shows (from left to right) Neil Kinnock, the leader of the Labour Party (see p. 50) at the time of the 1992 general election (see p. 50), Paddy Ashdown, the leader of the Liberal Democrats (see p. 50), and John Major, the leader of the Conservative Party (see p. 50) and prime minister (see p. 51). They are shown wearing fools' caps and are called April Fools, a reference to April Fools' Day and to the fact that the election was held on 9 April.

1. Which of the quotations do you agree or disagree with? Explain why.
2. What is your reaction to showing the leaders of the three main political parties as 'April Fools'?
3. Explain why you think the people who voted for the Loony Party did or did not waste their votes.
4. What do you think the motives might be for David 'Screaming Lord' Sutch to put himself forward as a candidate for parliament? What serious comment might he be making about politics and democracy?
5. Comment on the statement that "Politics is too serious a business to make fun of or be cynical about".
6. Carry out an opinion poll in your class about politics and discuss the results. You could start by asking the following questions:
   a) Does politics bore you? Why?
   b) Does it worry you that so many people are apathetic about politics? Why? Why not?
   c) Why do you think some people are bored with politics?
   d) Is there a single political issue which interests you? Which one is it and why?
   e) If political education is important what should be done to increase people's knowledge about politics and what do they need to know about politics?

1 | Excerpts from *Magna Carta**

Vocabulary

Intro/4 arbitrary (adj.): typical of power that is uncontrolled and used without considering the wishes of others - **5 count** (n.): a European nobleman with a rank similar to that of a British earl (see below) - **7 abbot** (n.): a man who is the head of a monastery (= a religious institution for monks) - **7 earl** (n.): a British nobleman of high rank - **8 justice** (n.): a judge in a law court - **8 forester** (n.): a person who works in or is in charge of a forest - **9 sheriff** (n.): the chief officer of the monarch in a county - **9 steward** (n.): a person who is employed to look after a house and lands - **10 official** (n.): a person who holds a public office - **15 to grant** (v.): to allow - **16 heir** (n.): /eə/ the person who has the right to receive the property of another person when that person dies - **22 consent** (n.): agreement or permission - **22 to hold** (v.): to possess land which is owned by the king - **24 scutage** (n.): /ˈskjuːtɪdʒ/ (archaic) tax paid by a knight to the monarch instead of doing military service, or money paid by a landowner instead of personal service - **24 aid** (n.): (archaic) tax paid to the monarch on certain occasions such as the marriage of a daughter - **24 to levy** (v.): /ˈlevi/ to demand and collect officially - **24 unless it be**: (archaic) unless it is - **25 ransom** (n.): a sum of money paid to free a prisoner who is being held illegally - **25 knight** (n.): a man of noble rank trained to fight esp. on horseback; a knight has the title Sir in front of his first name - **27 customs** (n.): taxes paid on goods entering or leaving a country - **28 borough** (n.): /ˈbʌrə/ town, or a division of a large town, with some powers of local government - **30 realm** (n.): /relm/ kingdom - **30 assessment** (n.): calculating or deciding the value of s.th. - **31 to cause** (v.): here to make; to force - **32 to summon** (v.): to order officially to come - **36 fee** (n.): here land - **37 due** (adj.): owed or owing as a debt or right - **38 offence** (n.): an act of breaking the law - **38 to fine** (v.): to take money from s.o. as a punishment - **39 to deprive s.o. of s.th.** (v.): to take s.th. away from s.o. - **39 livelihood** (n.): the job or way in which s.o. earns money to live on - **40 to spare** (v.): to not take s.th. - **40 merchandise** (n.): things for sale; goods - **40 husbandman** (n.): (archaic) farmer - **40 implement** (n.): tool - **41 husbandry** (n.): (archaic) farming - **41 to fall upon** (v.): (archaic) to find o.s. - **41 mercy** (n.): power to forgive or not to punish - **41 to impose** (v.): here to make (s.o.) pay - **42 oath** (n.): a solemn promise - **42 reputable** (adj.): /ˈrepjətəbəl/ having a good reputation, esp. for being honest - **43 obligation** (n.): duty - **45 cart** (n.): a two- or four-wheeled vehicle pulled by an animal, or pulled or pushed by hand - **49 corn** (n.): here wheat - **50 dyed** (adj.): given a different colour - **51 to place s.o. on trial**: to make s.o. (who is thought to be guilty of a crime) appear before a court of law to decide whether they are guilty or not - **51 unsupported** (adj.): without having any other facts to show the truth of what he is saying - **51 to produce** (v.): to bring before the public; to show - **52 credible** (adj.): deserving to be believed - **53 to seize** (v.): to arrest or capture by force - **56 to delay** (v.): to move to a later time

Explanations

Title Magna Carta (Latin): Great Charter, also called *Magna Charta*, a document signed by King John giving rights and privileges to the barons, church and freemen and which is traditionally regarded as the basis of English liberties - **Intro/1 King John**: (1166-1216), King of England (1199-1216) - **Intro/2 Petition of Right (1628)**: This petition limited the power of the monarchy by stating that the citizen has the right not to be taxed without the agreement of parliament. - **Intro/2 Bill of Rights (1689)**: see p. 49 - **3 Duke of Normandy**: Besides being King of England, John was also Duke of Normandy. Normandy, a part of northern France, had been in the possession of the English crown since William the Conqueror's invasion of England in 1066. - **4 Aquitaine**: /ˌækwɪˈteɪn/ region of southwest France - **5 Anjou**: /ɑ̃ˈʒu/ region in the west of France

Awareness

1. a) Working in groups decide what you think are the most basic freedoms and rights that people have in a democracy and place them in order of importance.
   b) Write short notes justifying your choice and their order.
   c) Compare your list with those of other groups and try to agree on a common list.

Comprehension

2. What do sections (12), (14), (15), (20), (39), (40) mean? Rewrite each section in your own words.
3. Place the clauses of *Magna Carta* under the following headings (some may fit under one or more headings, some may not fit under any): (a) consumer rights; (b) civil rights; (c) representation; (d) women's rights; (e) taxation; (f) powers of the king and government; (g) local government; (h) workers' and employees' rights; (i) the courts.
4. Compare your list of basic freedoms and rights with those listed in the extract from *Magna Carta*. How many can you find in both lists?

Analysis

5. From your reading of this excerpt from *Magna Carta*, what would you say were the wrongs and injustices which *Magna Carta* was intended to stop?

Opinion

6. Place the 14 points taken from *Magna Carta* in order of importance, starting with the one you consider most important. Compare your list with those of other students and justify your choice.

Project

7. Find out about the events which led up to the signing of *Magna Carta*. Kenneth O. Morgan, ed., *The Oxford History of Britain* (Oxford: Oxford University Press, 1990), and Christopher Haigh, ed., *The Cambridge Historical Encyclopedia of Great Britain and Ireland* (Cambridge: Cambridge University Press, 1990), will provide you with information.

Politics in Britain

2 Antony Jay
"A 'United' Kingdom: The Role of the Monarchy"*

Vocabulary

Intro/3 marital (adj.): relating to marriage - **1 hereditary** (adj.): which can be passed down from an older to a younger person, esp. in the same family - **4 to dissolve** (v.): to cause to end - **5 act** (n.): law - **8 to discharge** (v.): to perform (a duty) properly - **18 to engage** (v.): to attract and keep (the interest and attention) of (s.o.) - **21 to walk tall** (v.): to feel very confident - **30 neatly** (adv.): simply and effectively - **36 faction** (n.): a group or party within a larger group - **37 getting on for** (adv.): almost - **39 impartial** (adj.): /ɪmˈpɑːʃəl/ not giving special favour or support to any one side - **40 coronation** (n.): the ceremony at which a king or queen is crowned - **46 to confer** (v.): formal for to give - **56 constitutional** (adj.): allowed or limited by a political constitution (= the system of laws or principles, usually written down, according to which a country or organisation is governed) - **61 embodiment** (n.): s.o. that represents, includes, or is very typical of s.th. else - **71 to take for granted** (v.): to accept a fact or situation without questioning its rightness - **72 Yugoslavia**: /ˈjuːɡəʊˌslɑːvɪə/ - **82 sovereign** (adj.): /ˈsɒvrɪn/ in control of a country; ruling - **85 bygone** (adj.): past; former

Poem

far-flung (adj.): spread over a great distance - **to impose** (v.): to establish officially - **engrossed in** (adj.): so interested in that it takes all one's attention - **football pools** (n.): an arrangement by which people risk small amounts of money on the results of certain football matches, and those who guess the results correctly win large shares of the combined money - **Noel Coward**: (1899-1973); English dramatist, actor and composer, noted for his comedies

Satire
Satire from Latin *satira*, a later form of *satura* - a medley or plate filled with fruit - has been defined in a number of different ways but most critics agree that satire is the use of ironical and sarcastic humour to expose and ridicule the faults of society.

Awareness
1. Is it necessary to have a head of state at all? What is the distinction between a head of state and a head of government?
2. Working in groups make a list of the arguments for and against having a monarch as head of state. In making your list bear in mind the advantages and disadvantages of having a monarch as head of state as against a head of state elected by the people (as in the United States) or by a special assembly (as in Germany). Compare your list and comments with those of other students.

Comprehension
3. What arguments does the author put forward in support of the monarchy and against an elected president?
4. What two roles does the British monarch combine?
5. Why does the author write that the British monarchy is "not that undemocratic after all" (ll. 92-94)?

Analysis
6. Explain the contrast between public life as being like "a battlefield" (l. 31) and like "a family circle" (l. 32).
7. Examine the implications of the words "pride" (l. 18), "patriotism" (l. 18), "loyalty" (l. 19) and "affection" (l. 60) as used in this article. What values does the writer seem to attach to them? How can these values be justified?
8. What are the implications of the author's statement that "Democracy has to be balanced against continuity" (ll. 48-50)?
9. How does the writer try to persuade the reader that his arguments are correct?

Opinion

10 Give your opinion on the arguments made by the author in favour of a hereditary monarchy. How far did the author's arguments change or confirm your opinions?
11 What is a state if it is "more than a collection of individuals, a system of laws and an area of land" (ll. 13f.)? Write down your ideas and compare them with those of other students.
12 What is the "force [or forces] for unity" (ll. 68f.) in countries that do not have a monarch? Could these same forces apply in Britain, too?
13 What does the satirical picture of the royal family on p. 4 tell us about British opinion of the royal family?
14 What is your opinion of the satirical picture of the royal family and of similar attacks on other political and social figures?
15 Compare the article written by Antony Jay with the one written by Tony Benn (see information sheet 2). Which do you think is more effective? Justify your choice.

Projects

16 Read articles and books which support and attack the monarchy in Great Britain, summarise the arguments made for and against the monarchy and come to a conclusion: should the monarchy be abolished (= brought to an end by law) or not? Some books which deal with the monarchy and its place in British political and social life are J. Cannon and R. Griffiths, *The Oxford Illustrated History of the British Monarchy* (Oxford: Oxford University Press, 1988), T. Nairn, *The Enchanted Glass – Britain and its Monarchy* (London: Century Hutchinson Radius, 1988), E. Wilson, *The Myth of the British Monarchy* (London: Journeyman/Republic, 1989). For a light-heartedly satirical look at the royal family read Sue Townsend, *The Queen and I* (London: Methuen, 1992).
17 Hold a class debate in which two speakers propose the motion (= a formal suggestion made at a meeting) that "This house believes that the monarchy is a valuable and unifying institution" and two speakers oppose it. After opening the debate to the rest of the class, take a vote on the motion.

3 | The Myth of the 'Unwritten' British Constitution*

Vocabulary

Intro/4 error (n.): mistake - **statute** (n): a law passed by parliament - **to regulate** (v.): to control by rules or laws - **composition** (n.): the various parts from which s.th. is made up - **electorate** (n.): all the people in a country who have the right to vote - **sovereignty** (n.): /'sɒvrənti/ having the highest power in the country - **customary** (adj.): usual; established by custom - **appointment** (n): choosing s.o. for a job - **dissolution** (n.): ending of parliament before an election - **pardon** (n.): an official action forgiving a person for an illegal act and giving freedom from punishment - **award** (n.): s.th. given as a result of an official decision - **honours** (n.): (in Britain) special titles given as a sign of respect - **work** (n.): book; article - **convention** (n.): a generally accepted practice - **to operate** (v.): to make (s.th.) work; to put (s.th.) into practice - **to enforce** (v.): to cause to be obeyed - **to appoint** (v.): to choose for a position or job - **confidence** (n.): (in parliament) a majority of votes - **to assent** (v.): to agree to a suggestion or proposal - **to pass** (v.): to officially approve or agree to esp. after a vote

Explanations

Act of Parliament: a law made by parliament - **Representation of the People Acts 1832-1928**: These acts increased the numbers of the population who were allowed to vote from 438,000 in 1832 to the whole of the population over 21 in 1928. - **House of Commons**: see p. 50 - **House of Lords**: see p. 50 - **Parliament Act 1911**: This reduced the power of the House of Lords to change or delay bills (= proposals for new laws) sent up to that House by the House of Commons. - **Act of Union with Scotland 1707**: the law under which England and Scotland were united on 1 May 1707. Scotland was guaranteed 45 seats (MPs; see p. 51) in the House of Commons and 16 places in the House of Lords. The Scots accepted common taxation, currency and weights and measures and a common flag, the Union Jack, but kept their own legal system, based on Roman Law. The Scots parliament voted itself out of existence in January 1707 but only after its members had been paid to do so by England. - **Bill of Rights 1689**: see p. 49 - **European Communities Act 1972**: the law which enabled Britain to become a member of the European Economic Community on 1 January 1973 - ***Habeas Corpus* Act 1679**: see p. 50 - **royal prerogative**: see p. 51

Politics in Britain

Quotation

Mr Burke: Edmund (1729-97); British statesman and conservative political theorist; he was a Whig MP (see p. 51) from 1765-1794. In his opinion Britain had a constitution based on a continuity of values and on documents going back to *Magna Carta*. - **to produce** (v.): here to show; offer for examination - **Thomas Paine**: (1737-1809); English-born radical political thinker, later one of the leaders of the American Revolution. He rejected the idea that a constitution could be either unwritten or not contained in one single document.

Awareness
1. What is the function of a political constitution?
2. Write down those points you know that are contained in the German constitution. Check your answer using the actual document.

Comprehension
3. To which of the four parts of the British constitution: (a) statute and EU law, (b) common law, (c) works of authority, (d) conventions, do the following statements refer
   - the Queen has to agree to laws which have been passed (= officially approved by a vote) by the House of Commons;
   - the British parliament has supreme power in Great Britain;
   - certain groups of people are allowed and others are not allowed to vote in elections in Great Britain;
   - Thomas Erskine May wrote a book on parliamentary procedure in which he stated that in the House of Commons MPs should not call each other by their names but by the names of the areas that they represent;
   - the Queen decides which ministers shall be in the government but only on the advice of the prime minister;
   - a person can be kept in prison only for a limited period before appearing before a court of law;
   - Scotland is a part of the United Kingdom of Great Britain and Northern Ireland;
   - the monarch must choose a certain person to be prime minister;
   - the monarch can free someone from prison on the advice of the prime minister;
   - the House of Lords cannot stop the House of Commons from passing (= officially approving by a vote) laws.
4. Which parts of the British constitution are unwritten?

Opinion
5. Discuss the advantages and disadvantages of Britain's part-written and uncodified constitution?

Projects
6. Compare the German or the American constitutions, which are both set out in one document, with the British constitution, as described here. What similarities and what differences can you find?
7. Find out about and read some of the key documents and events of the British constitution. Describe their contribution to the British political system: 1628 Petition of Right; 1642-49 English Civil War; 1679 *Habeas Corpus* Act; 1689 Bill of Rights; 1832 Reform Act; 1967 Parliamentary Commissioner Act; 1970 Equal Pay Act; 1972 European Community Act; 1975 Sex Discrimination Act; 1976 Race Discrimination Act.

4 | Roger Woddis
"Helping with Enquiries"

Vocabulary

***Title* enquiry** (n.): question to obtain information; "helping (the police) with their enquiries" is a common phrase used by the police when s.o. is being held and questioned by the police about a crime, but not yet officially charged with the crime - **Intro/1 peasant** (n.): /'pesənt/ a person who works on the land, esp. one who owns and lives on a small piece of land - **Intro/2 plainclothes** (adj.): wearing ordinary clothes while on duty, rather than a uniform - **Intro/3 to incite** (v.): to cause or encourage (s.th.); to provoke - **6 in one's tracks**: suddenly; where one is at that moment - **7 serf** (n.): a farm worker, esp. in a feudal system, who has no rights; if the lord sold the land, the serf was passed on to the new landlord - **8 to stand one's ground** (v.): to refuse to accept defeat in an argument - **12 copper** (n.): (slang) police officer - **19 to caution** (v.): to give an official warning about s.th. bad already done - **20 to detain** (v.): to prevent a person from leaving for a certain time

Explanations

Intro/1 poll tax: a tax of a fixed amount collected from every citizen; a poll tax was introduced in England in 1381 which provoked the Peasants' Revolt (see below). It is also the name popularly given to the local tax, the community charge, introduced by Mrs Thatcher's (see p. 51) government first in Scotland in 1989 and then in England and Wales in 1990. It proved so unpopular (with riots in London and other cities) that it was stopped by John Major's government as soon as Mrs Thatcher left office. It was hated because the less well-off paid as much per head as the wealthy. Its replacement, the council tax, is based on the value of people's houses. - **Intro/1 Peasants' Revolt**: The immediate causes of the Peasants' Revolt, which took place in southeastern and eastern England, were the heavy and unfair burden of three poll taxes in the years 1377 to 1381 to finance a war with France and the oppressive behaviour of the tax collectors. Other longer-term causes were the inefficiency and corruption of government and hatred of restrictive labour laws which reduced peasant mobility and kept wages low. The revolt was led by Wat Tyler and a priest named John Ball. - **1 Wat Tyler**: also Walter, died 1381; he led the Peasants' Revolt from Kent to London where he tried to come to an agreement with King Richard II (1367-1400). He was killed by the Mayor of London, William Walworth, while the discussions between them were in progress. - **10 Smithfields**: now the name of the main meat market in London, situated to the northeast of the Tower of London; in 1381 Smithfields was open land. It was here where King Richard and Wat Tyler tried to come to an agreement and where Wat Tyler was killed.

Background Information

Rioting

The introduction of the poll tax, or community charge, caused some of the worst rioting seen in mainland Britain in the twentieth century. It also led to a widespread protest and civil disobedience movement which included all groups and political parties in the United Kingdom. Differences of opinion about the poll tax as well as about Europe within the Conservative Party led to Mrs Thatcher's downfall at the end of 1990.

The rioters and protesters continually made references to the Peasants' Revolt against poll taxes in 1381, in which one of the leaders, Wat Tyler, was killed. Since then rioting or political violence has played an important part in British history in either resisting illegitimate, unjust or repressive government actions or in attempting to bring about political change.

The tendency of the English to riot had been noted by visitors to England. Benjamin Franklin, wrote in 1769: "I have seen within a year riots in the country about corn; riots about elections; riots about workhouses; riots of colliers; riots of weavers; riots of coalheavers; riots of sawyers; riots of Wilkesites; riots of government chairmen; riots of smugglers, in which customs-house officers and excisemen have been murdered [and] the King's armed vessels and troops fired at." (Ian Gilmour, *Riots, Risings and Revolution: Governance and Violence in Eighteenth-Century England* (London: Hutchinson, 1992), p. 15.)

Franklin's list is relatively short. He could have added riots against turnpikes, enclosures and high food prices, against Roman Catholics, the Irish and Dissenters, against the naturalisation of Jews, the impeachment of politicians, press gangs, theatre prices, pimps, bawdy houses, surgeons, foreign actors, French footmen and alehouse keepers, against the Cider Tax and the Shops Tax, against workhouses and industrial employers, and even against a change in the calendar.

Further rioting occurred throughout the nineteenth century, some of the most serious in 1886, when a bitterly cold winter put many Londoners in the building trade and the docks out of work. A demonstration was organised in Trafalgar Square where a crowd of about 20,000 turned up. After speeches demanding employment, part of the crowd went in the direction of Pall Mall. Stones were thrown at the Carlton Club windows and then the crowd smashed windows of fashionable shops near Hyde Park and overturned a few carriages.

After the end of the nineteenth century there was a period of comparative calm until the youth riots in Brixton, London and Toxteth, Liverpool in 1981, when a large number of buildings were destroyed by fire.

Awareness
1. Think of some of the ways in which ordinary people can influence politicians and those in authority. Choose one of the following issues and, working in groups, decide in what ways you and other citizens could respond to them: (a) a local primary school which you attended and which your younger brother or sister now attends is to be closed because the authorities say there are not enough pupils to enable it to be run efficiently; (b) a large number of pupils and students cycle to school along a busy and dangerous road; a safe cycle track could be built alongside a railway track but the local authority say that it would be too expensive to build; (c) a proposal has been put forward to burn rubbish in a plant which will send out toxic fumes near where you live.

Comprehension
2. What do you learn about Wat Tyler and Dave Roddy from this poem? What do they have in common?
3. Who is "they" in line 11?
4. How was Wat Tyler treated by those in power?
5. How was Dave Roddy treated by those in power?
6. What were the differences in the treatment the two men received?

Analysis
7. How would you describe the tone of this poem? Choose one or more of the following terms and justify your choice: humorous, tragic, satirical, solemn, melancholic, sarcastic, ironical, comical, cheerful, enthusiastic, critical. What does the tone suggest about the poet's attitude towards Dave Roddy, Wat Tyler, the police, and the political situation in general?
8. Explain the poet's choice of title. Think of alternative titles and explain why you think they are suitable.
9. What are the implications of the last two lines: "But twenty million on the march/Can't all of them be wrong."

Opinion
10. Summarise your reaction to the poem in one sentence. Compare your reaction with those of other students.
11. The police methods described in the poem could be summarised as either 'maintaining law and order' or 'suppressing legitimate protest'. How far can citizens go in protesting against what they consider unjust state action and how far can the state go in preventing its citizens from protesting against the actions of the state?

Projects
12. Use suitable encyclopaedias to find out about one or more of the following popular political movements: (a) the Peasants' Revolt of 1381; (b) the Levellers (17th century); (c) the Luddites (early 19th century); (d) the Chartists (1830s and 40s); (e) the anti-poll tax movement of the 1980s.
13. Work out a campaign to influence the authorities for one of the cases mentioned in question 1.

5. How Representative is Parliament?*

Vocabulary

Title **representative** (adj.): typical of a system of government in which one group of people acts and speaks officially for the people - **Intro/1 satirical** (adj.): see p. 28 - **Intro/2 to subsidise** (v.): to pay part of the cost of s.th. for s.o. - **Intro/2 compulsory** (adj.): obligatory; which must be done by law, by orders - **Intro/3 performance** (n.): the ability of a person to do s.th. well - **Intro/3 bunch** (n.) informal for group - **Intro/3 self-opinionated** (adj.): too sure of the rightness of one's opinions - **Intro/4 windbag** (n.): (slang) a person who talks too much - **Intro/4 busybody** (n.): a person who takes too much interest in other people's affairs - **11 record** (n.): the known or recorded facts about the past behaviour or performance of a person - **15 to vote out** (v.): to choose a different MP at an election - **16 accountable** (adj.): having to give an explanation for one's actions - **17 seductively** (adv.): attractively - **19 to endorse** (v.): to express support of - **22 to reverse** (v.): to change to the opposite - **25 to legislate** (v.): to make a law or laws - **26 sovereign** (adj.): /ˈsɒvrɪn/ ruling, in control of - **28 to overrule** (v.): to decide against (s.th. already decided) - **34 tenuous** (adj.): insignificant; having little meaning or strength - **37 to modify** (v.): to change - **39 electoral system** (n.): system by which people are chosen for an official (esp. political) position by voting - **44 to cast** (v.): to make (a vote) in an election - **50 to reward** (v.): to give advantages or success - **51 disproportionately** (adv.): here too much in relation to (the votes they get) - **51 to penalise** (v.): to put s.o. in a very unfavourable or unfair position - **61 to delay** (v.): to move to a later time - **64 legislation** (n.): the act of making laws - **67 revision** (n.): changing s.th. - **67 amendment** (n.): making a change to improve a law - **76 hereditary** (adj.): /həˈredətəri/ (a title or position) which can be passed down from an older to a younger person in the same family - **84 to toe the party line** (v.): to obey the orders or rules of the party or group to which one belongs - **85 asset** (n.): valuable advantage - **86 to deviate** (v.): to be different or move away from a usual or accepted standard of behaviour - **91 to liken** (v.): to compare to - **94 virtually** (adv.): almost; very nearly - **94 to come round** (v.): to happen; to take place as usual - **98 to advance** (v.): to help; to improve - **100 agreeable** (adj.): pleasant - **101 dismissal** (n.): the act of being removed (from a job) - **111 expertise** (n.): /ˌekspɜːˈtiːz/ skill in a particular field - **112 guile** (n.): /gaɪl/ being clever in deceiving - **112 to outwit** (v.): to defeat by behaving more cleverly - **116 edifice** (n.): /ˈedəfɪs/ here complicated structure - **124 to promote** (v.): to gain or obtain support for - **125 cause** (n.): an idea, principle, or movement that is strongly supported - **128 fee** (n.): a sum of money paid for professional services - **131 extensive** (adj.): large in amount - **132 to diminish** (v.): to become smaller, reduced - **133 vital** (adj.): very necessary; of the greatest importance - **133 web** (n.): network

Explanations

Intro/1 BBC: British Broadcasting Corporation; the British radio and television company that is paid for by the state and not by advertisers. It was established in 1926. - **Intro/2 MP**: see p. 51 - **2 general election**: see p. 50 - **3 constituency**: see p. 50 - **12 Westminster**: see p. 51 - **50 first past the post**: see p. 50 - **78 peer**: member of the aristocracy who has the right to sit in the House of Lords (see p. 50), (one of the five noble ranks, baron, viscount, earl, marquis /ˈmɑːkwɪs/, duke) - **77 life peer**: see p. 51 - **78 law lord**: a member of the House of Lords who holds, or has held, a high position in the legal profession - **91 Lord Hailsham**: (1907-) a senior Conservative politician and member of the legal profession. Before becoming a peer his name was Quintin Hogg. - **96 prime minister**: see p. 51 - **102 backbenches**: any of the seats in the British parliament on which members who do not hold an official position in the government or opposition may sit; a member who sits there is called a backbencher. - **103 civil service**: see p. 50 - **114 chamber**: House of Commons (see p. 50)

Quotation

Thomas Carlyle: (1795-1881); a Scottish essayist and historian

---

Awareness

1. Working in groups write down what you know about the British and German political systems. Make notes on the following topics: (a) The electoral systems (How aften are general elections held? What voting systems are used?); (b) How are the upper chambers (House of Lords, *Bundesrat*) chosen? What are their functions?

Comprehension

2. In what ways does the writer show that the British people are imperfectly represented by the British electoral system?
3. What power does the House of Lords still have?
4. How does belonging to a political party affect the way MPs vote in parliament?
5. Why did Lord Hailsham refer to the British parliamentary system as an "elective dictatorship" (l. 91)?
6. In what ways does the civil service have power in the British political system?
7. Name the groups of people that MPs listen to.

Analysis
8 How far does the excerpt justify the statement made by Jim Hacker in the introduction?

Opinion
9 Give your ideas for remedying the faults in the British political system found by the writer.
10 The House of Lords consists of 1200 or so "non-elected people". What are the advantages and disadvantages of having such an undemocratic second chamber?

Projects
11 Find out about, describe, and compare the composition of second chambers in Great Britain, the United States and Germany.
12 Compare the role and powers of the British prime minister and the German *Bundeskanzler*.

6 | Jonathan Lynn and Antony Jay
"The Smokescreen"

Vocabulary

Intro/5 cunning (n.): cleverness in deceiving - **4 to cancel** (v.): to give up (a planned activity, event, etc.) - **10 smugly** (adv.): too pleased with o.s.; showing too much satisfaction with one's own qualities - **11 input** (n.): information that is provided to help s.th. succeed or develop - **12 announcement** (n.): a statement making publicly known what has happened or will happen - **13 implication** (n.): a possible later effect of an action, decision, etc. - **14 ramification** (n.): any of a large number of results that follow from an action or decision - **14 delaying** (adj.): intended to make s.th. take a longer time than it should - **20 juncture** (n.): /ˈdʒʌŋktʃə/ a particular point in time - **21 in due course**: at the right time - **25 to turn out to be** (v.): to happen to be in the end - **25 banana skin** (n.): an event or situation likely to cause difficulty or make one look foolish - **27 obstinacy** (n.): /ˈɒbstɪnəsi/ refusal to change one's opinion or behaviour - **27 to encounter** (v.): to meet; to have to deal with - **29 billion** (n.) one thousand million - **38 to acknowledge** (v.): /əkˈnɒlɪdʒ/ to accept; to admit - **43 to reiterate** (v.): /riːˈɪtəreɪt/ to repeat several times - **45 loftily** (adv.): showing that one thinks one is better than the other person - **49 to pitch for s.th.** (v.): to attempt to get - **50 to get away with s.th.** (v.): here to succeed in doing s.th. which other people do not like - **65 tempting** (adj.): attractive; making s.o. want to do s.th. - **65 to do away with** (v.): to take out of service - **71 source** (n.): a place from which s.th. comes - **77 lobby** (n.): a group of people who unite for or against a planned action in an attempt to persuade those in power to change their minds - **79 to eliminate** (v.): to stop completely - **86 progressive** (adj.): increasing continuously - **86 deterrent** (adj.): preventing s.o. from doing s.th. - **89 scheme** (n.): /skiːm/ a formal, official or business plan - **93 proposal** (n.): a plan or suggestion - **103 approval** (n.): agreement - **105 stalling** (adj.): see 'delaying' (l. 14 above) - **114 to secure** (v.): (formal) to get - **116 to make one's case** (v.): to give good arguments - **127 baffled** (adj.): confused - **131 revenue** (n.): income that the government receives as tax - **141 tense** (adj.): showing nervous anxiety - **147 derisively** (adv.): showing that s.th. cannot be taken seriously, that s.th. is foolish - **152 to prohibit** (v.): to forbid by law or rule - **154 to chuckle** (v.): to laugh quietly - **158 superior** (adj.): better in quality - **161 to contemplate** (v.): to think deeply about taking a course of action - **165 patronising** (adj.): /ˈpætrənaɪzɪŋ/ showing s.o. that one is better or more important than s.o. else - **168 sane** (adj.): healthy in mind; not mad - **171 footwork** (n.): ability to think very quickly in response to a situation - **172 to reverse** (v.): to change to the opposite - **177 novel** (adj.): new - **178 do-gooding** (adj.): intended to help people but naive and impractical - **183 to persist** (v.): to continue in a course of action in spite of opposition - **190 link** (n.): s.th. which connects two other parts - **195 reluctance** (n.): unwillingness, and therefore slowness to act - **201 hideous** (adj.): /ˈhɪdɪəs/ extremely shocking - **202 appalling** (adj.): /əˈpɔːlɪŋ/ shocking; terrible - **202 to go for the kill** (v.): here to give a final argument which destroys your opponent's argument - **203 fortune** (n.): a great amount of money - **211 to brief** (v.): to give s.o. information in order to prepare them for an activity - **213 to go into s.th.** (v.): to explain s.th. in depth - **218 rate** (n.): here number; quantity - **222 cholera** (n.): /ˈkɒlərə/ - **223 smog** (n.): /smɒɡ/ - **226 to withdraw** (v.): to take away - **231 flourishing** (adj.): /ˈflʌrɪʃɪŋ/ growing healthily

Explanations

Intro/1 BBC: British Broadcasting Corporation; the British radio and television company that is paid for by the state and not by advertisers. It was established in 1926. - **Intro/1 satire**: see p. 28 - **Intro/2 civil service**: see p. 50 - **2 study paper**: a short document written to examine whether a particular decision should be taken - **4 Trident**: a type of American missile which is fired from a submarine. Each Trident can send several nuclear explosive charges to different places. In 1982 the British government ordered Trident missiles to equip four nuclear submarines at a total estimated cost of £12 billion. - **5 conscription**: making people serve in one of the armed forces by law, usually in the form of national service, in which men serve in the armed forces for a limited period. Conscription was ended in Britain in 1958. Since then Britain has had professional armed forces. - **23 Parliament**: the period between the official opening of parliament after a general election and its official closing before the next general election, a period of at most five years - **27 Chancellor of the Exchequer**: /ɪksˈtʃekə/ see p. 49 - **33 Treasury**: the government department that is responsible for managing the money system of the country and for carrying out government plans in relation to taxes and public spending - **61 capital ship**: one of the largest and most heavily armed ships in a naval fleet - **63 Admiral of the Fleet**: the highest rank in the Royal Navy - **71 minister of state**: a person whose job is to help the minister who is the head of a government department; each department has one or two ministers of state, or junior ministers as they are sometimes called - **103 Bernard**: Bernard Woolley in the TV series *Yes Prime Minister* is Jim Hacker's secretary. He is a civil servant whose job is to manage the prime minister's private office. The role of this office is to help the prime minister prepare for parliamentary business and parliamentary questions and to assist with correspondence and advise about the work of other departments. - **203 NHS**: see p. 51 - **223 Public Health Act**: In the 19th century there were four cholera epidemics (1831-32, 1848-49, 1853-54, 1866) which killed about 140,000 people in England, Wales and Scotland. Although the precise virus which caused cholera had not yet been identified it was known that clean water and good sanitation prevented the disease. After the first cholera epidemic parliament passed (= officially approved by a vote) the Public Health Act of 1835, which required local authorities to build sewers (= large pipes under the ground to carry away water and waste material from human bodies), provide clean water, and to demolish unsanitary housing. - **224 Clean Air Act**: London had suffered badly from air pollution, largely from the burning of coal in domestic fireplaces ever since the 17th century. Various ineffective attempts were made to control pollution in the 19th century but it was not until the killer smog of December 1952 that the government took effective action and then only after a public outcry and a long campaign by the pressure group, the National Society for Clean Air. In fact the Clean Air Act, which made the burning of smokeless fuels compulsory, was not passed by parliament until 1956. The number of people killed in the 1952 smog given by Jim Hacker is, as one would expect, on the low side; other authorities estimate that it caused 4,000 premature deaths. - **232 balance of trade**: the difference in value between a country's imports and exports; not to be confused with balance of payments, the difference between the amount of money coming into a country and the amount going out, taking into account all international business such as trade in goods, services, insurance and banking

Quotation

saving grace (n.): the one good thing that makes s.th. acceptable - **Billy Bragg**: (1957-); Steven William; born in Barking, London; folk-rock singer and songwriter

Awareness

1 Working in groups discuss why many people are cynical about politics and do not trust politicians. If politicians changed their behaviour what consequences would this have?

Comprehension

2 Why does Jim Hacker want to cancel Trident and reintroduce conscription?
3 How will the Minister of State for Health help Jim Hacker get his tax cuts?
4 Why was it important that the Treasury should hear about Dr Thorn's plans to stop smoking?
5 Why is Sir Humphrey against Dr Thorn's plan to reduce cigarette smoking?

Analysis

6 What strategies does Sir Humphrey use to delay Jim Hacker's plan?
7 What is the point of Sir Humphrey's question to Jim Hacker: "What would happen to the British Navy, for instance?" (ll. 55f.)?
8 Why does Dr Thorn think that he should forget his plan to stop smoking after Jim Hacker had said that he agreed with him?
9 What is so brilliant about Jim Hacker's plan? In what way is it "a smokescreen" (l. 137)?
10 How does Jim Hacker know that Sir Humphrey is against his plan to raise taxes on cigarettes when he appears to support it?
11 Why does Jim Hacker mention the Public Health Act and the Clean Air Act (ll. 223f.)?
12 Find examples of Jim Hacker's and Sir Humphrey's cynicism.

Opinion

13 How far do you agree with the picture that is presented here of politicians and civil servants? Justify your view.

Project

14 Imagine you had a chance to confront both Jim Hacker and Sir Humphrey and criticise them for their cynicism. Formulate the statements and questions you might put to them and then add the replies that you might receive.

7 | The Story of the Tolpuddle Martyrs

Vocabulary

Title **martyr** (n.): /ˈmɑːtə/ - **Intro/1 founder** (n.): a person who starts an organisation - **Intro/2 to be transported** (v.): to be sent to a distant land as punishment - **Intro/2 sacrifice** (n.): giving up s.th. of value, esp. for what is believed to be a good purpose - **Intro/3 to sentence** (v.): (of a judge or a court) to give a punishment to - **Intro/4 oath** (n.): a solemn promise - **Intro/5 mutiny** (n.): the act of taking power from s.o. in authority - **2 lot** (n.): the quality of a person's life - **3 enviable** (adj.): /ˈenvɪəbəl/ very desirable - **9 outstanding** (adj.): very good; much better than most others - **11 progressive** (adj.): developing continuously or by stages - **12 to come to terms** (v.): to reach an agreement - **14 intermediary** (n.): a person who comes between two people or groups of people, esp. in order to bring them into agreement - **24 eruption** (n.): a sudden increase in activity - **25 to take fright** (v.): to be suddenly frightened - **26 rick** (n.): (also hay rick) a large pile of wheat stems or straw which stands out in the open air until it is needed - **27 magistrate** (n.): an official who judges cases before the lowest courts of law - **28 sought** (v.): past tense of the verb to seek - **28 guidance** (n.): help and advice - **29 upshot** (n.): the result in the end - **37 offence** (n.): act of wrongdoing, esp. breaking the law - **41 retaliation** (n.): the act of doing s.th. bad to s.o. who has done s.th. bad to you - **46 to take advantage** of (v.): to make use of - **47 charge** (n.): an official statement that s.o. is responsible for a crime - **61 trial** (n.): hearing and judging a person in a court of law - **62 to lodge** (v.): to give s.o. a place to live for a time - **63 to try** (v.): to hear and judge in court of law - **64 to pass a sentence** (v.): to state what punishment a criminal declared to be guilty in a court will receive - **70 to violate** (v.): to break; to act against - **72 reputation** (n.): an opinion held about s.o. - **75 utter** (adj.): complete - **75 degradation** (n.): losing one's self-respect - **76 starvation** (n.): suffering or death from not having enough food - **77 to challenge** (v.): to invite s.o. to do s.th. which is very difficult - **81 object** (n.): purpose; aim - **83 to operate on** (v.): (archaic) to have an effect on - **83 offender** (n.): s.o. who does s.th. wrong, against the law - **90 convict** (n.): /ˈkɒnvɪkt/ a person who has been found guilty of a crime and sent to prison, esp. for a long time - **98 harrowing** (adj.): causing great suffering - **99 chain gang** (n.): a group of prisoners chained together for work outside their prison - **102 serf** (n.): a farm worker, esp. in a feudal system, who has no rights; if the lord sold the land, the serf was passed on to the new landlord. - **107 lot** (n.): any of a set of objects of different sizes used for making a choice or decision by chance - **111 cause** (n.): a principle, aim or movement that is strongly defended or supported - **118 instigation** (n.): the action or responsibility for starting s.th. - **122 but** (adv.): only - **122 agitation** (n.): public action for or against political or social change - **125 pardon** (n.): an action of a court forgiving a person for an illegal act and giving freedom from punishment - **125 to see to** (v.): to deal with - **126 dependant** (n.): a person who depends on s.o. else for food, clothing, money, etc, usually the member of s.o.'s family - **127 subscription** (n.): an agreement to pay a sum of money - **132 to swear in** (v.): to cause to make a solemn statement of loyalty - **134 decorum** (n.): correct and respectful behaviour - **140 becoming** (adj.): proper or suitable - **143 release** (n.): being set free - **154 to propose** (v.): to put forward for consideration; to suggest - **158 ringleader** (n.): a person who leads others to do wrong or make trouble - **162 to amend** (v.): to make changes in the words of - **162 previous** (adj.): happening before the one mentioned

Explanations

Title **Tolpuddle**: a village in the county of Dorset in southwest England - **Intro/5 Mutiny Act**: (1789) after a number of mutinies in the British Navy this law made the taking of secret oaths illegal. It was then used to restrict trade union organisation. - **13 vicar**: (in the Church of England) a priest in charge of a district - **16 Grand National Consolidated Trade Union**: a trade union, one of whose leaders was Robert Owen, the aim of which was to destroy the capitalist system and organise society on a co-operative basis - **17 Robert Owen**: (1771-1858) the owner of textile mills in New Lanark in Scotland. He used the profits from his mills to benefit the workers and people of New Lanark by building a school, an institute and a community centre. - **21 Friendly Society**: a type of club which started in the 17th century and became increasingly popular in the 18th and 19th centuries in which workmen combined for the purpose of insuring against sickness, old age, or death. Each member paid in a weekly contribution to the club's fund, which was then used to pay members or their families when they needed help. At a very early stage friendly societies became rudimentary trade unions, since one of the uses to which their funds were put was as strike pay for striking members. - **28 home secretary**: see p. 50 - **29 Lord Melbourne**: /ˈmelbɔːn/ William Lamb, Viscount (1779-1848), home secretary 1830-34, prime minister (see p. 51) 1834, 1835-41 - **31 Dorchester**: the county town of Dorset in southwest England - **32 assizes**: a special court held in county towns by an important judge travelling from one county town to another; in 1971 the assize court system was ended and replaced by Crown Courts - **44 freemason**: a man belonging to a very old and widespread secret society, the members of which give help to each other - **45 Orangeman**: a member of a society which began as a secret order in Ireland in 1795 with the aim of upholding the Protestant religion, the Protestant royal family and Protestant supremacy against Catholics and Irish nationalists. The name is taken from William, the protestant prince of Orange in the Netherlands, who later became King William III of England. He was invited to become King of England to replace the Catholic king, James II. William defeated James's army at the Battle of the Boyne in 1690. The anniversary of this battle, the 12th July, is celebrated in Northern Ireland by Protestants as Orangeman's Day. - **38 Act of 1824**: the Combination Law of 1824 officially ended earlier laws (the Combination Acts of 1799 and 1800) which made the formation of an organisation for the purpose of increasing wages and changing working hours a criminal offence. After 1824 there was a great increase in trade union activity and it was at this time that the word union came into use to mean a workers' organisation. - **45 lodge**: a local branch of certain societies, esp. of Freemasons and Orangemen - **88 hulk**: the body of an old ship, no longer used at sea; hulks were used as prisons in the 18th and 19th centuries - **89 Portsmouth**: /ˈpɔːtsməθ/ a town in Hampshire in southern England, site of important naval dockyards - **91 New South Wales**: a state in southwestern Australia bordering on the Pacific Ocean - **96 Tasmania**: a large island forming a state of Australia, off its southeastern coast - **100 penal settlement**: a place, often on an island, where prisoners are kept - **120 Warwick**: /ˈwɒrɪk/ a town in central England - **120 London Radicalism**: a group of political thinkers and activists who wished to change the British political system completely. They were organised in the London Radical Reform Association and were influential in the 1830s. - **129 Copenhagen Fields**: /ˌkəʊpənˈheɪgən/ open land just north of the City of London - **130 King's Cross**: one of London's most important main line railways stations, built in 1852. It is now also an underground station. - **134 Whitehall**: the street in London in or near which most of the British government offices stand - **144 William Cobbett**: (1762-1835) from 1802 he published a number of political journals and newspapers in which he outspokenly criticised the evils in English society - **144 Joseph Hume**: (1777-1855) started out a conservative but became an advocate of radical change in England. He helped secure the official ending of the anti-trade union Combination Acts of 1789 and 1800 in 1824 (see above). - **145 Thomas Wakley**: (1795-1862) a surgeon (= doctor who performs medical operations), social and medical reformer who entered parliament in 1835 and whose first speech there was in support of the Tolpuddle Martyrs - **150 Commons**: the House of Commons (see p. 50) - **153 Lord John Russell**: (1792-1878) an MP (see p. 51) belonging to the Whig Party, later renamed Liberal Party (see p. 50); besides being home secretary he also held the office of secretary of war, prime minister, and foreign secretary (see p. 50).

Awareness
1 What does the word 'martyr' mean to you? Can you think of any martyrs in history?
2 Would you be prepared to suffer for your political and religious beliefs? If not, why not? If you were prepared to suffer, how far would you be prepared to go? Would you risk losing your job, being forced to emigrate, suffering imprisonment, undergoing physical hardship?

Comprehension
3 Why was the life of an agricultural worker in the 1830s particularly difficult?
4 What was the reason the court gave for sentencing the Tolpuddle Martyrs to transportation?
5 What was the real reason?
6 Why was it possible to imprison the Tolpuddle Martyrs even though they had done nothing illegal?
7 What reasons did the men who had formed a union give for their actions?
8 What was done to help the men's families while they were in Australia?
9 What means did the supporters of the Tolpuddle Martyrs use to obtain their release?

Analysis
10 What view is presented here of (a) the trade unionists; (b) the authorities?

Opinion
11 Some people argue that trade unions were necessary in the 19th century to fight the very bad working conditions of that time, but that with all the improvements which have taken place over the years, they are no longer needed now. What is your opinion?

Projects
12 Produce a role play of the trial of the Tolpuddle Martyrs at the Crown Court, in which you take the parts of the lawyers who prosecute and defend the men, the accused (George and James Loveless), witnesses for the prosecution and the defence, and the judge. Write role cards for each of the participants giving brief notes on what they should say.
13 Find out about and write a report on the lives of working people in England from the beginning of the 19th century to the present day. The following books will be of help: William Cobbett, *Rural Rides* (Harmondsworth: Penguin, 1988) (first published in 1830; it is a unique survey of southern England and the life of agricultural workers, with comments on education, economics and social policy). J. B. Priestley, *English Journey* (London: Mandarin, 1994) (first published in 1933; it describes Priestley's travels to both rural, urban and industrial areas gripped by the Great Depression. It expresses his anger at the waste of so many lives through unemployment and the degradation caused by the Industrial Revolution). George Orwell, *The Road to Wigan Pier* (Harmondsworth: Penguin, 1962) (first published in 1937; it describes the poverty in a northern English city and the dangers posed by both fascism and communism).

Politics in Britain

8 | "Should We Ban Strikes in Key Public Services?"

Vocabulary

Intro/2 disruption (n.): bringing or throwing into disorder - **Intro/3 issue** (n.): a subject to be talked or argued about - **3 record** (n.): the known facts about the past behaviour or performance of a person or group - **5 hostage** (n.): a person who is kept as a prisoner by an enemy so that the other side will do what the enemy demands - **6 to settle** (v.): to end; to bring to an agreement - **17 to impose** (v.): to establish officially - **17 statutory** (adj.): fixed or controlled by law - **19 legislation** (n.): a law or set of laws - **24 industrial action** (n.): action by workers (such as strikes) intended to put pressure on employers to agree to the workers' demands - **25 one-off** (adj.): happening or done only once - **26 unilateral** (adj.): done by or having an effect on only one side - **28 deal** (n.): agreement - **28 to provide for** (v.): to make the necessary future arrangements for - **29 arbitration** (n.): the settling of an argument by the decision of a person or group that has been chosen by both sides - **29 last-resort** (adj.): done if everything else fails - **29 option** (n.): a course of action that is possible and may be chosen - **30 maintenance** (n.): the act of keeping s.th. in good condition - **34 substantially** (adv.): quite a lot - **39 to outlaw** (v.): to declare s.th. not legal - **40 feature** (n.): a typical or noticeable part or quality - **40 high-profile** (adj.): the state or quality of attracting a lot of attention - **43 sinister** (adj.): threatening; suggesting evil or unpleasantness - **43 shift** (n.): a change in position or direction - **45 to back off** (v.): to accept defeat in an argument - **45 to implement** (v.): to carry out; to put into practice - **46 outline** (adj.): not in a detailed form - **46 on the stocks**: in preparation - **47 to shackle** (v.): here to restrict or limit s.o.'s freedom - **48 wanting** (adj.): lacking; not existing - **48 stumbling block** (n.): s.th. which prevents action - **49 application** (n.): putting s.th. to use - **51 smooth** (adj.): free of problems - **51 running** (n.): control; management - **54 to encompass** (v.): to include - **59 to compound** (v.): to make worse by adding to or increasing - **59 scope** (n.): range or area of action - **61 to enforce** (v.): to cause s.th. to be obeyed - **62 to contemplate** (v.): to think deeply about taking a course of action - **62 offender** (n.): s.o. who breaks the law - **64 impact** (n.): the strong effect (of s.th.) - **65 to eradicate** (v.): to put an end to - **66 exploitation** (n.): using s.o. unfairly for profit or advantage - **71 prerequisite** (n.): s.th. that is necessary before s.th. else can happen or be done - **74 to negotiate** (v.): to talk to another person or group in order to try to come to an agreement or settle an argument - **76 stick** (n.): (slang) severe criticism - **79 to impose on** (v.): to force the acceptance of - **81 case** (n.): good arguments that support the opinions of one side in a disagreement - **86 to play upon** (v.): to try to use or encourage (esp. the feelings of others) for one's own advantage - **88 blackmail** (n.): the influencing of s.o.'s actions by threats, causing anxiety, etc. - **91 to roll in** (v.): (slang) to arrive - **93 convenor** (n.): a member of a committee whose duty is to call meetings - **93 council** (n.): the organisation responsible for local government in a town or county - **94 cremation** (n.): burning the body of a dead person - **96 horrendous** (adj.): really terrible - **105 redundancy** (n.): being made unemployed - **112 crucial** (adj.): /ˈkruːʃəl/ of deciding importance - **113 constituent** (n.): see p. 50 - **114 distressing** (adj.): causing great suffering of the mind - **116 barrister** (n.): a lawyer who has the right of speaking in the higher courts of law - **126 conscription** (n.): making s.o. serve in the armed forces or do work by law - **129 plant** (n.): factory - **130 restraint** (n.): s.th. which prevents s.o. from doing s.th. - **137 to maintain** (v.): to argue (in favour of s.th.) - **138 at the end of the day**: when everything is considered - **142 marginalised** (adj.): caused to become unimportant

Explanations

12 legal immunity: trade unionists who go on strike have special legal protection. They cannot normally be taken to court for the consequences of their strike action. - **23 tort**: a wrongful act that is dealt with in a civil court, i.e. a court concerned with private conflicts between people and with the rights of private citizens rather than criminal cases - **41 public sector**: those industries and services that are run by the state - **73 general secretary**: the union official responsible for the day-to-day running of the union - **74 EEPTU**: Electrical, Electronic, Telecommunications and Plumbing Union, now combined with the Amalgamated Engineering Union to form the AEEU, Amalgamated Engineering and Electricians Union, with over 800,000 members - **80 Margaret Thatcher**: see p. 51 - **84 Pulp**: the name of a pop group - **93 GMB**: a union representing over 800,000 manual workers; originally GMB stood for General Municipal and Boilermakers, now it is just the name of the union - **97 1979**: the period in the winter of 1978-9 known as Winter of Discontent in which many strikes occurred in protest against the Labour government's attempts to limit pay rises. It helped the Conservative Party (see p. 50) under Mrs Thatcher win the general election (see p. 50) in 1979. - **108 Tory**: a member of the British Conservative Party - **125 Mussolini**: Benito, (1883-1945) an Italian Fascist dictator, known as Il Duce. He became prime minister of Italy in 1922 and assumed dictatorial powers. He annexed Abyssinia (now Ethiopia), allied Italy with Germany in 1936, and entered World War II in 1940. He was killed by Italian partisans after the war.

Cartoon

clocking-on (n.): recording the time when one arrives at work on a special card

Awareness
1 What do you understand by "key public services"?

Comprehension
2 What does Ira Chalphin mean by "an out-dated system of settling industrial disputes" (ll. 5f.)?
3 In which industries would Ira Chalphin like to see strikes banned?
4 What is, for Ira Chalphin, the main difference between key public services and other services?
5 Why, according to Roger Poole, has the government not introduced laws to ban strikes in key services?
6 What course of action would Roger Poole like the government to take, rather than banning strikes?
7 Which of the people in "Views" support, and which oppose the banning of strikes in key public services?

Analysis
8 What are the main arguments put forward by Ira Chalphin in support of a ban on strikes in key public services?
9 What are the main arguments used by Roger Poole to oppose a ban on strikes in key public services?
10 How valid and convincing are the arguments used by Ira Chalphin and Roger Poole?
11 Find one sentence in each article which sums up the writer's argument. Justify your choice.

Opinion
12 Write a critique of one of the two main articles in which you criticise the writer's arguments and put forward your own views. Compare your criticisms and views with those of other students.

Projects
13 Think of some of the ways in which government policies and political decisions can affect the lives of people at work - for the better, and for the worse.
14 *Case study and role play*: This case is about young workers in a bank, but it could apply to almost any workplace.

Background: Joe/Jeanette is a union representative for the Union of Bank Workers. He/She has been elected by the staff at the Allied Bank and takes up their problems with the manager. Alan/Angela is a bank clerk at the Allied Bank and is a member of the Union of Bank Workers. He/She has been asked to see the manager. He/She thinks he/she is going to be punished for an incident that happened yesterday with a colleague (Stephen/Susan).
The bank has rules which its staff must obey. These are:
 i) The manager has the right to punish a member of staff for committing an offence.
 ii) There are two types of offence that will be punished:
    a) small offences (e.g. being late or not working properly)
    b) serious offences (e.g. fighting, vandalism, stealing)
 iii) Possible punishments are:
    a) You get a warning in writing.
    b) You are not allowed to work and get no pay for a week.
    c) You are dismissed (= removed from your job).
 iv) Staff may ask their union representative to represent them in talks with the manager.

Procedure: Work in groups of four. Each student plays one of the four roles: Joe/Jeannette (union representative), the bank manager, Alan/Angela (bank clerk), and Stephan/Susan (colleague).
 1) There is a meeting between Joe/Jeanette, the union representative, and Alan/Angela in which he/she tells the union representative about the incident and about the meeting with the bank manager.
 2) The union representative talks to Stephen/Susan.
 3) There is a meeting between the union representative and the bank manager.
 4) There is a final meeting between the bank manager, the union representative and the employee in which the bank manager says what he has decided to do.

Politics in Britain

Joe/Jeanette, the union representative's role card

- You are the union representative for the Bank Workers' Union at the Allied Bank.
- Alan/Angela, one of your members, has come to see you and says that he/she has been asked to see the manager.
- He/She thinks the manager is going to punish him/her for an incident that happened yesterday.
- You must find out as much as possible about the incident so that you can help your colleague.

The bank manager's role card

- Last night after work you heard a lot of shouting in the car park. You went outside and saw Alan/Angela hit Stephen/Susan.
- You are thinking of dismissing Alan/Angela. The bank's rules allow you to dismiss anyone who commits a serious offence.
- You believe you have to be firm with the people who work in the bank so that they do their work properly, and give the bank a good name.
- However, you have agreed to see Joe/Jeannette, the union representative, to discuss what should happen to Alan/Angela.

Alan/Angela's role card

- You tell the union representative about the incident.
- You borrowed a coat from another employee, Stephen/Susan, at the bank.
- While you were wearing it you fell over and tore the lining. It was a small tear and you had it repaired.
- When you returned the coat you showed the tear and apologised. But your colleague was angry and did not accept the apology. He/She said you had damaged the coat deliberately.
- You talked to the colleague about this after work.
- When Stephen/Susan saw you waiting for him/her after work he/she said nothing but just pushed past you.
- You lost your temper and hit out at Stephen/Susan.
- The manager walked by at that moment and saw the incident.

Stephen/Susan's role card

- You rather unwillingly lent your coat to Alan/Angela because it was new.
- You are very angry that your coat wasn't looked after.
- You suspect that Alan/Angela is envious of your new coat and damaged it deliberately.
- It wasn't repaired very well.

Discussion after the role plays:
Discuss the decisions that the bank managers came to. Were they fair? Justify your opinion.

9 | Political Advertising*

Vocabulary

Conservative advertisement

billion (n.): one thousand million - **to suspect** (v.): to believe (esp. s.th. bad) to be true - **mortgage** (n.): /ˈmɔːgɪdʒ/ an amount of money lent esp. so as to buy a house - **incentive** (n.): s.th. which encourages s.o. to greater activity - **to cripple** (v.): to damage, weaken seriously - **demand** (n.): the desire of people for goods and services

Labour advertisement

condition (n.): an illness - **to affect** (n.): to cause some change in - **surgeon** (n.): /ˈsɜːdʒən/ a doctor whose job is to perform medical operations - **due** (adj.): expected or supposed (to happen) - **to admit** (v.): to permit to enter - **to cancel** (n.): to give up (a planned activity) - **cardiac** (adj.): connected with the heart or heart disease - **intensive care unit**: a department in a hospital which gives special attention and treatment to people who are very seriously ill - **emergency** (n.): an unexpected and dangerous happening which must be dealt with at once - **relief** (n.): feeling of comfort at the end of anxiety - **ventilator** (n.): an apparatus for pumping air into and out of the lungs of s.o. who cannot breathe properly - **to slip away** (v.): to go or leave unnoticed - **to regain** (v.): to get back

Explanations

NHS: see p. 51 - **Fallot's Tetralogy**: also called tetralogy of Fallot; a fault in the heart which is there from birth; from Etienne Fallot, the French doctor who named the disease in 1888 - **Great Ormond Street**: a famous children's hospital in London - **Norman Lamont**: (1942-) Conservative MP (see p. 51), chancellor of the exchequer /ɪksˈtʃekə/ (see p. 49) from November 1990 to May 1993

Quotations

Alan Coren: (1938-); English humorist and writer - **enamoured** (adj.): very fond of - **as distinguished from**: in contrast to - **Liberal**: here progressive; left-wing - **Ambrose Bierce**: (1842-?1914); American humorist and writer

Awareness
1. Think of reasons why political advertising is effective or not.

Comprehension
2. What reason(s) does the Conservative Party advertisement put forward for not voting Labour and for voting Conservative?
3. What reason(s) does the Labour Party advertisement put forward for not voting Conservative and for voting Labour?

Analysis
4. What fundamental differences are there in the messages of the two advertisements?
5. Explain how each poster tries to achieve its aim of persuading the reader to vote Labour or Conservative.

Opinion
6. Which of the two advertisements shown in the reader is more effective? Justify your opinion.

Projects
7. Imagine you are the copywriter who designed either the Labour or the Conservative advertisement. Explain the thinking and intentions which lay behind your choice of layout, pictures and wording.
8. Find out as much as you can about the policies of the three main political parties: Conservative, Labour, and Liberal Democrat. In which areas do they differ most; in which areas are they most similar? Election manifestos can be obtained from the head office of all three parties. Further information on their policies can be found in Robert Garner and Richard Kelly, *British Political Parties Today* (Manchester: Manchester University Press, 1993).

Politics in Britain

9. Before designing political advertisements some market research is necessary. One aspect of this research will be to find out the support given by the public to different political ideologies, philosophies and values. The most common classification is the 'left' – 'centre' – 'right' continuum, but this is rather too simple. Most political scientists also use a vertical axis to find out how democratic or authoritarian people are.

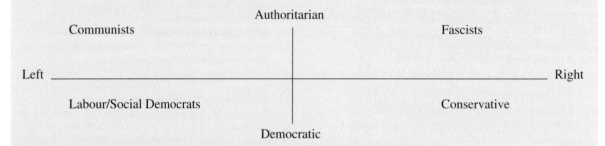

Work out a questionnaire which would enable you to carry out a market research survey of political attitudes. The questionnaire could take the following form:

Make statements about political issues and use the scale

6 = strongly agree
5 = agree
4 = not sure but probably agree
3 = not sure but probably disagree
2 = disagree
1 = strongly disagree

for the answers.

1. I am in favour of very strict enforcement of all laws no matter what the consequences.
2. The government should always be obeyed.
3. A period of military service is a good influence on most young men.
4. People should take more responsibility for their own welfare and not depend on the state.
5. Hanging should be introduced for murder.
6. It's the duty of all citizens to support their country, right or wrong.
7. If people are unemployed it's usually their own fault.
8. Comprehensive schools tend to lower educational standards.
9. The police should be given more powers to fight crime.
10. The churches and religion should have more influence in political life.
11. People are basically bad; society cannot make people better than they really are or improve on human nature.
12. Trade union power is too great. In the national interest it should be reduced.

You could draw up similar questionnaires about: (a) taxation; (b) education; (c) unemployment; (d) privatisation; (e) the environment; (f) crime; (g) defence and then design an advertisement to appeal to different types of voters.

10 "Portrait of the Electorate"

Explanations

Con: Conservative Party (see p. 50) - **Lab**: Labour Party (see p. 50) - **L/D**: Liberal Democrats (see p. 50) - **AB-prof**: AB professional; this group comprises a wide range of occupations. At the top are professional people such as accountants, architects, chemists, company secretaries, barristers, solicitors, senior civil servants, doctors, who have high status because of their educational qualifications. It also includes successful business people such as the self-employed and managers and executives of large companies. Then come other employers, senior managers and administrators. Finally there are middle managers, teachers, farmers. Note: the categories used in the chart are those devised by the British Market Research Society. - **C1-white collar**: this group comprises small tradespeople and shopkeepers, non-manual workers, office and administrative workers doing routine work, often referred to as 'white-collar' workers - **C2-skilled**: this group is made up of skilled manual workers, technicians, foremen and supervisors - **DE-semi- and unskilled**: the D group are workers whose skills are no longer useful (deskilled), who have only been partly trained and cannot therefore perform specialised work (semi-skilled) and who are untrained or do a job for which training is not necessary (unskilled); the E group are the poorest people in society: pensioners, the unemployed, people living on social security, and casual workers (= workers employed for a short period of time only) - **owner occupier**: s.o. who owns and lives in their house or flat - **council tenant**: s.o. who lives in a house or flat owned by the local council, the organisation responsible for the local government of a town, a district, or a county - **private tenant**: s.o. who pays rent to a private landlord, the owner of the house or flat in which they live - **m**: male; man - **f**: female; woman - **North**: the region in England north of Nottingham as far as the Scottish border - **Midland**: the region in England around Birmingham, and extending as far north as Nottingham - **South**: the region south of the Midlands, including London - **homeowner** (n.): s.o. who owns their own house or flat - **middle-class**: this comprises categories AB and C1 in the chart. - **working-class**: this comprises categories C2 and D in the chart.

Cartoons

Con: Conservative Party - **Lab**: Labour Party - **Lib Dem**: Liberal Democrats - **opinion poll** (n.): an attempt to find out the general opinion about s.th. by questioning a number of people chosen by chance - **distortion** (n.): a false or dishonest account of s.th. - **evasion** (n.): an attempt not to tell the whole truth - **outright** (adj.): complete - **polling booth** (n.): a partly enclosed space inside a building where people vote in an election where s.o. marks their voting paper secretly - **to poll** (v.): to question people

Awareness
1 Working in groups discuss which groups in Germany you think vote for which parties. Bear in mind the following groups: unskilled and skilled working class, middle class, men, women, members of trade unions, people who live in different parts of the country, people who rent a house or a flat, people who own a house or a flat.

Comprehension
2 How did the voting behaviour of men and women differ in the 1992 election?
3 In which of the age groups, 18 to pensioner, did more people vote for the Labour Party than for any other party in the 1992 election?
4 In which of the groups in the chart was support for the Liberal Democrats greater than for the Labour Party in the 1992 election?
5 In which of the groups in the chart was support for the Labour Party greatest in the 1992 election?
6 In which of the groups in the chart was support for the Conservative Party greatest in the 1992 election?
7 In which of the groups in the chart did support move most to the Labour Party between the 1987 and 1992 elections?
8 In which groups did the Conservatives and in which groups did the Liberal Democrats lose most votes to Labour between the 1987 and 1992 elections?

Analysis
9 Summarise the main trends in the voting behaviour of the British electorate from 1987 to 1992.
10 In what ways do the voting patterns of different age groups, sexes, social and regional groups differ?
11 What voting behaviour and patterns, if any, strike you as surprising? What explanations can you offer for them?

Opinion

12 If you were an adviser to the three main parties what strategies would you advise them to adopt to appeal to and gain more support from different social groups in the light of this chart?
13 What do the cartoons tell us about people's attitudes to politics and electioneering? Compare them with the quotations on p. 1. Which do you agree or disagree with? Justify your opinion.

11 | "Electoral Reform: Which System Is Best?"*

Vocabulary

Intro/1 ballot box (n.): the box into which the ballot paper, the sheet of paper used to make a secret vote, is put - **1 agenda** (n.): /əˈdʒendə/ a list of subjects to be dealt with - **2 fringe** (adj.): far from the centre - **5 overall majority**: a majority over all the other parties - **9 wistfully** (adv.): thoughtfully and rather sadly because s.o. wants s.th. that they will find difficult to get - **13 to cast** (v.): to make (a vote) in an election - **13 in s.o.'s favour**: for s.o.; in support of s.o. - **20 surplus** (n.): (an amount) additional to what is needed - **22 member** (n.): Member of Parliament (see p. 51) - **24 overall** (adj.): including everything - **26 hurdle** (n.): a barrier which must be jumped over - **38 to share out** (v.): to divide up and give out to s.o. - **40 to emerge** (v.): to come out or appear - **41 reinforced** (adj.): /ˌriːɪnˈfɔːst/ strengthened - **46 to abandon** (v.): to give up or bring to an end

Explanations

Intro/2 first past the post: see p. 50 - **8 proportional representation**: (also PR) a system of voting in elections by which all political parties, small as well as large, are represented in parliament according to the proportion of votes they receive - **15 single transferable vote** (STV): This system of proportional representation involves large constituencies (see p. 50) each of which elects between four and eight MPs. There will therefore be a large number of candidates on the ballot paper (= paper used for secret voting), probably at least 15 and perhaps as many as 30. STV has several advantages. The proportion of seats a party gets is very close to the proportion of votes cast (= made in an election) for it. Almost every vote counts, since first preference votes (= votes for the candidate you most wish to be elected) are redistributed as second preferences to help elect other candidates. Its disadvantages are that constituencies would not have one member and would be very large. - **17 constituency**: see p. 50 - **17 MP**: see p. 51 - **22 additional member system** (AMS): The advantage of this system is that it gets the best of both worlds: a bit of the first past the post system and a bit of PR. The disadvantages are that it is not clear whom the additional members represent; a hurdle has to be raised to prevent extremist parties getting seats in parliament; and for the first time in Britain, belonging to a political party is given official recognition as a qualification for being an MP. - **28 list system**: In this system voters vote for a party rather than an individual which makes its operation relatively simple. The votes for each party are counted and seats awarded to the parties in proportion to the share of the total vote that each party obtained. Depending on how the system is operated there can be various sizes of constituencies, hurdles to keep out small parties, and an MP for voters to lobby. - **33 alternative vote** (AV): Like single transferable vote, the voter puts numbers against the candidates in order of preference. Any candidate getting more than 50 per cent of the first preference votes wins automatically. If nobody has 50 per cent, the least-favoured candidate drops out and votes are redistributed to others according to second preferences. This process of removing the bottom candidate and redistributing votes continues until one of the survivors has more than 50 per cent. The advantage of AV is that single-member constituencies remain. The big disadvantage, as Australia has found, is that this system still doesn't prevent a party getting a much higher proportion of seats than of votes. - **34 lower house**: in parliaments and law-making bodies with two houses or chambers, the lower house is the more powerful and more representative body. In Britain the lower house is the House of Commons (see p. 50) and the upper house is the House of Lords (see p. 50). In Germany the lower house is the *Bundestag*, the upper house is the *Bundesrat*. - **Scottish National Party**: see p. 51 - *Plaid Cymru*: /ˌplaɪd ˈkʌmri/: see p. 51 - **Ulster Parties**: see p. 51

Quotation

blame (n.): responsibility for s.th. bad - **Laurence J. Peter**: (1919-); Canadian educator and co-author of the book The Peter Principle, according to which members in a hierarchy rise to their own level of incompetence

Cartoon

John Major (on the left): (1943-) a British politician in the Conservative Party (see p. 50) who entered parliament in 1979 and became prime minister (see p. 51) and leader of the Conservative Party in 1990 when Margaret Thatcher (see p. 51) resigned. Before becoming prime minister he had been chancellor of the exchequer (see p. 49) and foreign secretary (see p. 50) - **Neil Kinnock** (on the right above): (1942-) a British politician and leader of the Labour Party from 1983 to 1992 when he resigned after Labour lost the 1992 general election - **Paddy Ashdown** (on the right below): (1941-) a British politician and leader of the Liberal Democrats (see p. 50) since 1988 - **43 p.c.**: 43 per cent of the votes in the 1992 general election - **53 p.c.**: 53 per cent of the votes in the 1992 general election; the Labour Party received 36 per cent and the Liberal Democrats received 17 per cent of the votes.

Awareness
1 Working in groups describe how the German system for electing the *Bundestag* works.

Comprehension
2 Why are some European countries considering adopting Britain's first past the post voting system?
3 What is the point of proportional representation (PR)?

Analysis
4 What are the weak and strong points of the voting systems described here? Use the chart under the article and the explanations in the Study Aids to help you write your answer.

Opinion
5 What point does the cartoon (p. 20) make about the British electoral system?

Project
6 Form groups representing the Labour, Conservative, Liberal Democrat and Scottish National Parties. Draw up a statement for your group's party presenting its views on electoral reform, and giving reasons for supporting a particular electoral system.

12 An Interview with John Major: What do the Conservatives Stand for?*

John Major (1943-), a politician in the Conservative Party (see p. 50), entered parliament in 1979 and became prime minister (see p. 51) and leader of the Conservative Party in 1990 when Margaret Thatcher (see p. 51) resigned. Before becoming prime minister he had been chancellor of the exchequer /ɪks'tʃekə/ (see p. 49) and foreign secretary (p. 50).

After leaving school at sixteen, John Major worked at several jobs, including labouring, and was unemployed for a short period. At the age of 21 he joined a bank as a trainee. After working in Africa he returned to Britain and became personal assistant to Lord Barbour, chancellor of the exchequer from 1970 to 1973. He became active in local politics at this time and then in 1979 he entered parliament as MP for Huntingdon, a small town with a population of 16,540, situated in a rural area to the northwest of Cambridge. After holding several junior posts in Mrs Thatcher's governments he became foreign secretary in July, 1989, and then three months later chancellor of the exchequer.

Vocabulary
3 to tie in with (v.): to have a close connection (to) - **4 basics** (n.): fundamentals; the parts or principles on which everything else rests - **15 artificial** (adj.): not genuine; not real - **17 to sustain** (v.): to keep in existence over a long period - **22 to entrench** (v.): to establish firmly - **25 decade** (n.): a period of ten years - **25 expenditure** (n.): spending - **29 term** (n.): a fixed or limited period of time - **34 long-term** (adj.): over a long period of time - **43 disparity** (n.): being completely different or unequal - **55 courtesy** (n.): polite behaviour; good manners - **55 obedience** (n.): doing what one is ordered to do - **56 no-nonsense** (adj.): practical and direct - **56 distinction** (n.): clear difference - **59 novel** (adj.): new - **64 to take for granted** (v.): not to recognise the true value of s.th. - **64 to neglect** (v.): to give too little attention to - **65 to operate on** (v.): to use - **68 smack** (adv.): directly; precisely; right - **71 to propose** (v.): to suggest - **75 assault** (n.): (a) violent attack - **76 cohesion** (n.): /kəʊ'hiːʒən/ state of sticking together - **88 to benefit** (v.): to gain advantage - **89 gap** (n.): an empty space between two objects or parts of an object - **92 bogus** (adj.): intentionally false - **116 regimentation** (n.): controlling s.o. (firmly and strictly); forcing s.o. to obey orders - **118 overwhelmingly** (adv.): to a very great extent; in most cases - **121 to reinforce** (v.): /ˌriːɪnfɔːs/ to strengthen - **126 orderly** (adj.): peaceful and well-behaved

Explanations
Intro/3 Naughtie: /'nɒxti/ - **21 health reforms**: reforms introduced by the Conservative government to make the health service more efficient and cost-effective - **37 back to basics**: a slogan invented by the Conservative Party in 1993 - **93 poverty line**: a level of income under which a person or family is considered to be very poor and able to receive government help - **95 income support**: a payment made by the government to people who do not have enough money to live on, e.g. the old, low-paid or unemployed - **127 school rules**: most British schools have a more or less formal catalogue of rules which regulate pupils' clothing and behaviour in school.

Awareness

1. Imagine you had the chance to interview a politician. Write down a list of questions that you would ask him or her. Compare your list with those of other students.

Comprehension

2. What is, for John Major, the problem with social security?
3. How do James Naughtie and John Major see the economic situation in Great Britain over the last ten or fifteen years?
4. What does John Major mean by a classless society?
5. How does John Major want to improve education?

Analysis

6. What criticisms of John Major and his government are implied in James Naughtie's five questions?
7. What strategies does John Major use to answer and avoid the implied and open criticisms in the questions?
8. What is implied when John Major talks about "health reforms" (l. 21) and "social security changes" (l. 24)?
9. What are the implications of the "back to basics" (l. 37) slogan?
10. What is implied by saying that certain values are "instinctive to the British" (l. 53)?
11. What is meant by those who interpret a classless society as "some grey conformity" (l. 100)?
12. Explain the two different concepts of discipline mentioned by John Major.
13. What, according to John Major, are the achievements and aims of his government?

Opinion

14. Working in groups discuss John Major's statement that "the welfare state is sustainable over the long term" (l. 32). Include the following points in your discussion: (a) What is the welfare state? (b) What should the state pay for and what should the citizen pay for? (c) How far should people who are well-off be excluded from the welfare state?
15. John Major says that the gap between the poor and the better-off has not widened in recent years. Do you agree or disagree with him? Give reasons for your opinion.
16. Write a brief comment on John Major's thoughts about education, in which you carefully justify your agreement or disagreement with his views.
17. In what ways could a classless society in which "everybody, wherever they may come from, whatever they may start with, will have the same opportunities to progress as other people who perhaps start from quite different circumstances" (l. 103-106) be created? Or do you think that a classless society is utopian. If so justify your opinion.
18. Does John Major give a convincing performance? Give reasons for your answer.

13 A Political Speech: Tony Benn on Britain and Europe*

Tony (Anthony Wedgwood) Benn (1925-) was elected a Labour MP (see p. 51) for Bristol in 1950. When his father, the Viscount Stansgate died in 1960 he inherited the title and so became a peer (= member of the aristocracy who has the right to sit in the House of Lords (see p. 50), one of the five noble ranks, baron, viscount, earl, marquis /mɑːkwɪs/, duke). His seat was declared vacant since he then became a member of the House of Lords and was no longer allowed to sit in the House of Commons (see p. 50). However, he fought the following by-election (= a special election held between regular elections to fill a position whose former holder has left or died), won it but was not allowed to enter the Commons. He was responsible for a law which made it possible for people to give up their peerages (= noble titles), and was re-elected to his old seat. In the 1960s he was minister of power and minister of technology in the 1964-1970 Labour government. In the Labour government of 1974-1979 he was minister for trade and industry and then minister for energy. When a referendum was held in 1975 on whether Britain should stay in the European Community Tony Benn campaigned against Britain's membership. He lost his Bristol seat in 1983 but was then elected MP for Chesterfield.

Politics in Britain

Vocabulary

Intro/4 treaty (n.): an agreement between countries - **5 summit** (n.): a meeting between heads of government - **5 proposal** (n.): a plan or suggestion - **5 to bring forward** (v.): to introduce or produce for examination - **5 to convert** (v.): to change - **11 consent** (n.): agreement or permission - **12 effect** (n.): here operation - **18 eve** (n.): the time just before an important event - **18 negotiation** (n.): a discussion with other people in order to try to come to an agreement - **20 bold** (adj.): brave; not afraid to take risks - **20 office** (n.): a position of power in the government - **21 objective** (n.): aim - **26 degree** (n.): a certain amount of - **26 to emerge** (v.): to come out of - **30 to urge** (n.): try very hard to persuade - **31 member** (n.): Member of Parliament (see p. 51) - **33 cause** (n.): a principle or aim that is strongly defended or supported - **35 recognition** (n.): acceptance as being true - **44 constituent** (n.): see p. 50 - **47 to remove** (v.): to get rid of - **48 creche** (n.): /ˈkreʃ/ a place where babies and small children are cared for while their parents work - **55 bloodshed** (n.): the flowing of blood or killing people - **62 ballot** (n.): system of voting in which the vote is marked on a piece of paper which is put in a box and later counted - **75 to sack** (v.): to fire from a job - **77 to slope off** (v.): to go away in order to avoid doing s.th. you should do - **78 apathy**: /ˈæpəθi/ - **81 turnout** (n.): the number of people who vote in an election - **93 ballot box** (n.): box into which the pieces of paper on which people mark their votes are put

Explanations

Intro/1 MP: see p. 51 - **Intro/1 constituency**: see p. 50 - **Intro/1 Chesterfield**: an industrial and mining town in northern central England; population 70,000 - **Intro/4 Maastricht Treaty**: an agreement between the twelve countries of the European Union to become closer in their political, economic and monetary policies. It was agreed in the town of Maastricht in the Netherlands in December 1991. - **2 European Economic Community**: the original name of the European Union - **24 Single European Act**: an agreement in 1986 between the heads of government of the countries of the European Union to allow free movement of people, goods and services within the European Union - **30 referendum**: a direct vote by everyone to decide about something on which there is strong disagreement, instead of the government making the decision. Tony Benn is here referring to the 1975 referendum on Britain's continuing membership of the European Union, of which he was one of the main supporters. At that time Margaret Thatcher (see p. 51) opposed the demand for a referendum. When the Maastricht Treaty was signed she supported demands for a referendum. - **31 Right Honourable**: a title of respect used when addressing or mentioning important government or ex-government ministers - **31 Finchley**: the constituency in north London which Mrs Thatcher represented from 1959 until 1992 - **32 member for Yeovil**: Paddy Ashdown (1941-), the leader of the Liberal Democrats (see p. 50) from 1988, and the MP for Yeovil in southwest England - **37 front benches**: the front row of seats in the House of Commons (see p. 50). The term here applies to the members of the government and the leaders of the opposition parties who occupy them. - **56 Callaghan**: /ˈkæləhən/ Lord (James) (1912-), a Labour politician who was prime minister (see p. 51) from 1976 to 1979 - **56 Wilson**: Lord (Harold) (1916-1995), a Labour politician who was prime minister from 1964 to 1970 and from 1974 to 1976 - **57 Right Honourable lady**: Margaret Thatcher - **57 internal processes**: here actions taken within the Conservative Party - **58 Huntingdon**: John Major (1943-), MP for the constituency of Huntingdon (1979-) and prime minister (1990-). Huntingdon is a small town with a population of 16,540, situated in a rural area to the northwest of Cambridge. - **61 Chartist**: the members of a reform movement in England from 1838 to 1848 which demanded votes for all men, payment of MPs, constituencies of an equal size and secret voting - **61 Suffragette**: a female member of the movement which demanded votes for women at the beginning of the 20th century - **64 white person**: here a small group of people who take responsibility for governing a large number of other people - **65 1832**: the Reform Act of 1832 almost doubled the number of people allowed to vote in elections from 438,000 to 720,000. But this still meant that the vast majority of the population aged 20 and over (10.2 million people) was not allowed to vote. - **66 royal prerogative**: see p. 51. The royal prerogative is, according to Tony Benn, being used for the first time since 1649. - **68 Crown**: the monarch. Tony Benn means that the prime minister is using the royal prerogative so that his actions do not need to be discussed in parliament. - **87 Strangeways**: a prison in Manchester where prisoners took control and did much damage in 1990 as a protest against poor conditions in British prisons. After these disorders conditions were improved. - **90 Treaty of Rome**: an agreement made in 1957 between Belgium, France, West Germany, Italy, Luxemburg, and the Netherlands, which established the European Economic Community

Quotation

Churchill: Sir Winston (1874-1965); an English politician who was prime minister of Britain during most of the Second World War. He was prime minister again from 1951-55 - **electioneering** (n.): the work of persuading people to vote for a political party by visiting voters, making speeches, etc.

Awareness
1 Write down as many reasons as you can think of why politicians make speeches.
2 What is it that makes a good public speaker?

Comprehension
3 Who is Tony Benn referring to when he talks about "we" in "... that we should move first from the original membership through the European Act into something stronger." (l. 23)?
4 What is the meaning of the "it" that people are being more cautious and less-critical about when he says: "...when we discussed it 20 years ago, were more uncritical about it." (l. 27)?
5 What, according to Tony Benn, is the difference between the people who govern the European Union and those who govern Britain?
6 Why does Tony Benn say that the struggle to get a secret vote was a waste of time?
7 What are the three things that will, according to Tony Benn, happen when people realise that they can no longer influence the people who run the European Union?

Analysis
8 What is the central message of this speech and its supporting arguments?
9 Analyse the structure of Tony Benn's speech. How does it contribute to getting his message across?
10 Describe the tone of the speech. What words and expressions help to create this tone?
If you are able to see the video describe the contribution of Tony Benn's tone of voice, facial expressions and gestures to the effect of the speech.

Opinion
11 Write a letter to Tony Benn in which you give your views on what he said in his speech about Britain and Europe.
12 Write a speech in which you give your opinion on a political topic.
13 Look at the criteria you listed in answer to question 2. Is Tony Benn a good public speaker?

Project
14 Using books, British newspapers and magazines find out as much as you can about British views on the European Union. Find out about differences of opinion within the British political parties. Compare opinions about Europe in Britain and Germany.

14 "A Democratic Checklist"*

Vocabulary
Intro/1 panel (n.): a group of people who are chosen to perform a particular service - **5 consistency** (n.): the state of always keeping to the same principles or course of action - **6 inevitable** (adj.): certain to happen - **7 weighting factor** (n.): an amount added to some figures in statistics because of special factors - **8 to take account of** (v.): here to give importance to - **8 famine** (n.): extreme lack of food for a very large number of people - **14 participation** (n.): the taking part in an activity or event - **15 franchise** (n.): the right to vote in a public election esp. one held to choose a parliament - **15 turnout** (n.): the number of people who vote in an election - **18 citizenship** (n.): the rights you have when you belong to a particular country - **23 case** (n.): all the facts and arguments that support the opinions or claims of one side in a discussion or disagreement - **27 judiciary** (n.): /dʒuːˈdɪʃəri/ all the judges in the courts of law, considered as one group, and forming one of the parts of government - **27 arbitrary** (adj.): typical of power that is uncontrolled and used without considering the wishes of others - **27 torture** (n.): the act of causing s.o. severe physical pain as a punishment, or to force s.o. to give information - **28 association** (n.): the act of joining together in groups for a shared purpose - **28 residence** (n.): the place where one lives - **29 reasonable** (adj.): fair; acceptable to most people - **29 to facilitate** (v.): to make easy

Explanations
Intro/5 Benin: a republic in west Africa, formerly known as Dahomey, with a population of 2.27 million. Its official name is People's Republic of Benin.

Quotation
Bernard Levin: (1928-); English writer and journalist

Awareness
1 What are in your opinion the characteristics of a democratic political system?

Opinion
2 Why are free and fair elections not sufficient conditions to create a democratic political system?
3 Why do you think that Great Britain is, according to this checklist, less democratic than Germany?
4 Do you think that the criteria in the text for judging how democratic a country is are sufficient? Can you think of criteria that are not mentioned here?

Projects
5 To what extent can the British electoral system regarding the election of
(a) head of state, (b) head of government, (c) parliament (House of Commons and House of Lords) be regarded as free and fair? (See texts 3, 5 and 11)
6 Examine the British electoral system and state whether it fulfills the criteria of
(a) wide franchise, (b) real participation in the electoral process, (c) high turnout, (d) an atmosphere where political questions are openly discussed, (e) an education system that encourages participation and citizenship. (See texts 10 and 11)
7 Compare the British and German political systems using the criteria given in the checklist. In which areas is each country more or less democratic than the other?
8 Put forward concrete proposals for making the British political system more democratic.

Glossary

Bill of Rights, 1689: this law ended the long struggle between the monarchy and parliament by ensuring the supremacy of parliament. Monarchs now no longer ruled by divine right but owed their position to parliamentary vote. It also affirmed many other basic principles of constitutional liberties: The monarch had no say in parliamentary debates and the election of MPs, parliaments should be held frequently, and the executive alone cannot suspend laws.

cabinet: the cabinet is chosen by the prime minister and comprises about 20 senior ministers including the chancellor of the exchequer (see below), the home secretary (see below), the foreign secretary (see below), the leader of the House of Commons (responsible for organising the business of the House of Commons; see below), the leader of the House of Lords (responsible for organising the business of the House of Lords; see below), the secretaries of state for Scotland (head of the Scottish Office; responsible for education, health, agriculture, and planning in Scotland), Northern Ireland (head of the Northern Ireland Office; responsible for law and order, housing, education, health, and economic planning and development in Northern Ireland) and Wales (head of the Welsh Office; responsible for health, housing, education and economic planning and development in Wales), the secretary of state for trade and industry, the secretary of state for health, the secretary of state for social security, the secretary of state for the environment, the secretary of state for defence, the secretary of state for education and employment, the lord chancellor (head of the legal system in England and Wales), the minister of agriculture, fisheries and food, the secretary for national heritage (responsible for the arts, the media, historical buildings, the national lottery), and the secretary of state for transport. It is the highest decision-making body in the British political system.

chancellor of the exchequer /ɪksˈtʃekə/: the minister in the British government who is head of the Treasury, responsible for managing the money system of the country and for carrying out government plans in relation to taxes and public spending

civil service: all the various departments of the British national government except the armed forces, law courts and religious organisations. A civil servant is a person employed by the civil service.

Conservative Party: developed out of the Tory Party, which goes back to the late 17th century. It has dominated British politics in the twentieth century. Since 1945 it has been in power from 1951-1964, 1970-1974, and 1979- and has won eight of the thirteen elections held from 1945 to 1992. It has gained most from the first past the post system (see below) in recent years, since, with a divided opposition, 42% of the vote has been enough to ensure a Conservative majority in the House of Commons (see below).

constituency: (also called a seat) a political administrative district where voters elect a single MP (see below) to represent them in the House of Commons; the United Kingdom is now divided into 651 constituencies, which means that 651 MPs are entitled to sit in the House of Commons. The figure of 60-65,000 voters per constituency is only an average. In practice the number of voters per constituency varies widely. The Western Isles, one of the largest in geographical area has the smallest number of voters, 23,000, whereas one of the smallest in area, the Isle of Wight, has the largest number of voters, 99,000.

constituent: a voter; a person who lives in a constituency (see above)

first past the post: (also first-past-the-post) the voting system used in British national and local elections in which the candidate who gets more votes than any other wins the election. The winner does not need to have more votes than the losers have together; it is also called the simple majority system.

foreign secretary: the minister in the British government who is head of the Foreign Office and is responsible for relations between Great Britain and other countries

general election: an election in which all the voters - British subjects over the age of 18 except peers, people in mental homes, people serving a prison sentence of over one year, people found guilty of corrupt practices in elections - choose who will serve in the House of Commons (see below) and which party will form the government. The main political parties choose a candidate to fight for a seat in each constituency. People therefore usually have four or five candidates to choose from, each representing a political party. People vote by putting a cross by one of the names on the ballot paper (= the paper used for secret voting). The person who is elected for each constituency (see above) is the one who gains the most votes in that constituency (see "first past the post" above). The longest time that a parliament can run, i.e. the longest time between two general elections, is five years, but the prime minister (see below) can decide to call an election at any time in this period. Prime ministers usually call elections when they think the government has a good chance of being re-elected.

***Habeas Corpus* Act 1679**: under this law s.o. in prison has the right to appear in a court of law within a certain period of time so that the court can decide whether they should stay in prison.

home secretary: the minister in the British government who is head of the Home Office and is responsible for law and order, justice and immigration. A similar minister in a foreign government is usually called the minister of the interior.

House of Commons: it is the more powerful of the two parts of parliament, the other being the House of Lords (see below), the members of which are elected by citizens over the age of 18 at general elections (see above). Each member of the House of Commons represents the people in a particular area, a **constituency** (see above), and is their MP (see below). The House of Commons has 651 members. When a new law is introduced, it is passed first in the House of Commons, then sent to the House of Lords to be discussed and approved. Finally, it must be approved by the monarch.

House of Lords: it is the less powerful of the two parts of the British parliament. Its 1,202 members are not elected but have membership of the House of Lords because of their noble title, or because they have been given a noble title. Members of the House of Lords include lords, bishops, life peers (see below), and law lords (= people who have held a high position in the legal system and have been made members of the House of Lords).

Labour Party: was established after the 1906 election to represent working class interests and carry out social reforms not supported by the Liberal and Conservative parties. By 1924 it had enough MPs (see below) to form a minority government. In 1940 it became a part of the wartime coalition government under Winston Churchill. In the 1945 election at the end of the second world war it won power with a large majority and introduced a major programme of social and economic reform, including the setting up of the National Health Service (see below), the nationalisation of the coalmines, the steel industry and road transport, and the giving of independence to India, Pakistan, Burma, and Sri Lanka. In the 1980s it was weakened when many former Labour supporters broke away to form the Social Democratic Party.

Liberal Democrats: this party goes back to the Whigs in the 17th century, who changed their name to Liberal Party in the 1830s. After being in power for long periods in the 19th century it lost its position as the second main party to the Labour Party in the

1930s. From 1945 to 1979 it never managed to gain more than 13 seats at a general election (see above). As the third national party it is the main loser under Britain's first past the post system (see above).

life peer: a Briton who has the rank of peer but is not allowed to pass it on to a son or daughter after death. Until 1968 all members of the House of Lords (see above) were the sons or daughters of lords. Life peers were introduced in an attempt to improve the House of Lords. They are chosen by the government, with suggestions from the opposition parties, for their legal, political or social experience.

MP: Member of Parliament; a person who has been elected to represent a constituency (see above) in the House of Commons (see above). There are 651 MPs. They have a wide variety of duties and responsibilities. They deal with problems on behalf of their constituents (see above), which may be connected with housing, jobs, tax, pensions, or social security payments; they promote the interests of their constituency (see above) by trying to get orders for local industry, for example; they take their party's side in the battles between the political parties; they look carefully at the laws which are put before parliament; they monitor the activities of the government and the civil service (see above); and they may represent a number of special interests - trade unions, industries and regions.

NHS: the National Health Service; the NHS provides medical treatment for everyone and is paid for out of taxes and national insurance. Apart from the cost of medicine and drugs prescribed by a doctor, medical treatment by a doctor or at a hospital is free.

Plaid Cymru /ˌplaɪd ˈkʌmri/: (Welsh for Party of Wales) the Welsh Nationalist Party was formed in 1925 to secure self-government for Wales. It won its first seat in 1966 and obtained four seats in the 1992 general election (see above), all in the Welsh-speaking northwest of Wales.

Scottish National Party: was founded in 1928 and wants full independence for Scotland within the European Union. It gained its first seat in the House of Commons in 1969. In the 1992 election in spite of obtaining 21% of the Scottish vote it won only three of Scotland's 72 seats in parliament.

Thatcher, Margaret: (1925-), now officially Lady Thatcher. She was born Margaret Roberts, the daughter of a grocer in Grantham, Lincolnshire. She studied chemistry at Oxford University and later law. In 1951 she married Denis Thatcher, a wealthy businessman. She became leader of the Conservative Party (see above) in 1975. Under her leadership the Conservative Party won three general elections (1979, 1983, 1987). She was replaced as leader of the Conservative Party and prime minister in 1990 by John Major (1943-).

prime minister: British prime ministers have enormous powers. A prime minister:
a) is leader of the majority party in parliament;
b) is head of the government;
c) selects cabinet ministers;
d) appoints other members of the government, about 100 non-cabinet ministers;
e) may move ministers from one post to another;
f) may dismiss (= remove s.o. from their job) cabinet ministers or ask them to resign;
g) is chairperson of the cabinet (see above) and some other important cabinet committees;
h) co-ordinates government policy;
i) is the nation's chief spokesperson in national and international affairs;
j) is responsible for party discipline;
k) appoints more than 180 offices (judges and Church of England posts), appoints new members of the House of Lords (see above);
l) is political head of the civil service (see above);
m) through the royal prerogative (see below) can sign treaties (= agreements with other countries) and declare war.

royal prerogative: these are powers which are still, in theory, exercised by the monarch. They include the choice of prime minister, assent (= agreement) to legislation, the dissolution (= ending before an election) of parliament, the declaring of war and the making of treaties (= agreements with other countries). In practice most of these powers have passed to the prime minister, including the declaring of war and the making of treaties and some powers, such as assent to legislation, choice of prime minister and dissolution of parliament, are governed by convention. The royal prerogative enables the prime minister to declare war and make treaties without parliament having any say.

Ulster parties: These can broadly be divided into two groups: unionist parties, i.e. those which support and wish to maintain the Union with Great Britain, and nationalist parties, i.e. those which want closer links with the Republic of Ireland. In the first group, which tend to be supported by the Protestant community, are the Ulster Unionist party, the Democratic Unionist Party, the Popular Unionist Party, and the Progressive Unionist Party. In the second group, which are mainly supported by the Catholic community, are *Sinn Fein* /ˌʃɪn ˈfeɪn/ (Irish for we ourselves) and the Social Democratic and Labour Party. The Alliance Party is an attempt to bridge the gap between these two conflicting aims.

Westminster: refers to the Houses of Parliament (House of Commons and House of Lords; see above), from the district in London where they are situated.

Acknowledgements

We are grateful to the following for permission to reproduce copyright material:

Texts

"A 'United' Kingdom: The Role of the Monarchy",
taken from *The Monarchy*, ed. Laura Murrell,
© London Weekend Television 1992: pp. 3f.

"Helping with Enquiries" by Roger Woddis,
© *New Statesman & Society*, London 1990: p. 6

"How Representative is Parliament?"
taken from *Is Democracy Working?*,
ed. Sheila Browne, © Tyne Tees Television,
Newcastle 1986: pp. 7f.

"The Smoke Screen"
taken from *Yes Prime Minister*
by Jonathan Lynn and Antony Jay,
© BBC Worldwide Ltd., London: pp. 9ff.

"The Story of the Tolpuddle Martyrs",
© Trades Union Congress,
London 1991: pp. 11ff.

"Should We Ban Strikes in Key Public Services?",
© *The Observer*,
London 1994: pp. 14f.

"Portrait of the Electorate",
© *The Sunday Times*,
London 1992: p. 18

"Electoral Reform: Which System is Best?",
© *The Guardian*,
London 1992: pp. 19f.

"What Do the Conservatives Stand for?",
© BBC Worldwide Ltd.,
London 1994: pp. 21f.

"A Democratic Checklist",
© *New Statesman & Society*,
London 1994: pp. 23f.

Photographs and Illustrations

BBC, London: p. 9

Paul Curry, London: p. 15 (bottom)

Central Office of Information, London: p. 2

dpa, Frankfurt: pp. 7, 21

Focus, Hamburg: p. 6 (bottom)

The Guardian, London: p. 20 (bottom)

Hulton Deutsch Collection,
London: pp. 6 (top, middle), 13 (bottom)

The Independent, London: pp. 1, 19 (bottom right)

The Observer, London: p. 19 (top left)

PA News, London: pp. 3, 15, 23

R.C.H.M.E., London: p. 8

Rural History Museum, Reading: p. 11

Marion Schweitzer, München: p. 4 (bottom)

Cover photograph by:

Gareth Boden, Hertford

We should be very grateful for any information which might assist us in tracing the copyright owners of sources we have been unable to acknowledge.